G000245605

Bookshop Ltd,
Bromyard,

My Father,

A. G. STREET

PAMELA STREET

My Father, A. G. STREET

ROBERT HALE & COMPANY • LONDON

First Published in Great Britain May 1969
Reprinted June 1969
Reprinted September 1969
Reprinted November 1969

SBN 7091 0833 8

Robert Hale & Company
63 Old Brompton Road
London S.W.7

Printed in Great Britain by
Clarke, Doble & Brendon

To the Memory
of
My Father

"It is our duty to serve our land faithfully, so that when we die it may receive us in honour and not in shame."

A.G.S. *Land Everlasting*

FOREWORD
by
SIR ARTHUR BRYANT

When in 1966 my old friend Arthur Street slipped away to the other side of the hill I had seen little of him for many years. There is nothing like being, even in the humblest way, what is called a 'public' man for breaking up old acquaintanceship, since it is inherent in the life of a writer, lecturer or journalist—and A. G. Street and I were each of us all three—that new acquaintanceship is for ever breaking in on old. Except for an occasional interchange of letters and an odd public dinner at which we were both engrossed in the isolating business of making speeches, we had become almost strangers to one another; we both had our tasks of professional scribbling, and of farms to look after into the bargain, though his farm, of course, was far more distinguished than mine. Yet, like thousands of others, I read him every week in the *Farmers Weekly* and, every time I did so, renewed my memories of the big, friendly, forthright Wiltshireman who began to put English farming on the map of the modern townsman's mind at a time when the latter was almost a complete blank, bearing, like the medieval cartographer's maps of Africa, in place of knowledge the words, "Here be picnic sites!" "Here be bluebells to pick!" "Here be dangerous cows that may be bulls!"

Well, A. G. Street helped to change all that. In a very real sense, he is the direct ancestor of the "Archers" and all the innumerable persons, real and fictitious, who on radio, television and in the newspapers, serve to make an urban community farm-conscious. Unlike the little evacuee in 1940, we all know now that the milk on our doorstep does come out of "a dirty old cow" and not just out of a glass bottle, though comparatively few visualize what it means to milk, tend and feed a herd of cows on cold, dark, winter mornings and evenings when every pipe is frozen or every gateway on the farm a river of knee-high mud.

Arthur Street's first book, *Farmer's Glory*, was something of a phenomenon when it appeared in 1932 at the very nadir of British farming between the wars. It came out a year after my own *Charles II* and led to our first meeting; for I wrote to tell him the impact it had made on me and to congratulate him on his beautiful, direct and Cobbett-like English. At that time I was Educational Adviser to the Bonar Law Adult Education College at Ashridge, and I suggested that he should come and lecture there in some of our periodic agriculture courses, which he did with great success and distinction. It was the essence of the man that he was very much at home in that friendly place where men and women of every age, class and locality met in pursuit of a common understanding of public life and democratic affairs. To be a 'good mixer', as Arthur Street so essentially was, was the cardinal Ashridge virtue. Indeed the college grace, "For food and fellowship, thank God", might have been written for him, for it was these two commodities that he spent his life producing; food from his Wiltshire acres to feed his countrymen, and fellowship in every line of his many books and thousands of articles: racy, sensible, humorous, poetic, prejudiced, and essentially friendly and human. Like Cobbett, Borrow and Surtees, the three classic English writers with whom he had most in common, he was, above all, a humanist. Though a modest man—for nature had taught him to be so—he was never afraid to wear his heart on his sleeve, and, for all his outspoken dislikes, it was the most warm and friendly of hearts.

At the time he died he and I must have been writing our respective columns, he in the *Farmers Weekly* and I in the *Illustrated London News*, longer than almost any other living columnist, for we had each been at it without a break for thirty years. But while I was free to range over almost every subject under the sun, he was tied to a single theme, that of farming. Yet such was the wisdom, humanity and genial power of the man that his weekly page was never monotonous or repetitive, and seemed to range all nature: everything that walked, swam, flew or grew—animal, vegetable or human—was grist to his mill and to that probing, inquiring and enjoying pen.

Yet of all that he has written, now that he is what we call dead—and his writings, thank Heaven, are not dead and are little likely to be—the work of his to which my mind instinctively recurs is his first, *Farmer's Glory*. Its theme was twofold: to remind his readers, in an age when English farming was almost bankrupt, of the kind of farming Englishmen had done from time immemorial and were still doing when he was a boy; and to affirm his faith, in the teeth of near-failure and all discouragement, in man's eternal duty to the soil and the necessity of serving it with love and understanding, though to one's own financial hurt. Of the first he wrote:

> The farming was on a settled definite system, the result of centuries of experience. The arable land was divided into four fields of one hundred acres each. . . . The rotation was as unanswerable as the law of the Medes and the Persians. One always knew what crop a particular field would be growing two or three years ahead and worked to that end. Any slight variation was considered a sin, and, like sin, it always left its mark. For instance, if one were tempted to seed a piece of vetches or clover, the extra robbing of the ground showed in the ensuing wheat-crop. It mattered not a whit that the produce of this immoral seeding might bring in more money than a good crop of wheat. One didn't farm for cash profits, but one did one's duty by the land.

It was not only of land, crops and animals that Arthur Street wrote in his book; it was of men, the men whose age-long breeding and training had created the rural England of the past that had manned the ships at Trafalgar and the squares at Waterloo and made the loveliest and best-tended countryside of all the rich and lovely lands of Europe. I still recall the picture of his shrewd farmer father, "the organizer," and his aphorism that two boys on a farm together did half as much work as one and three none at all; his method of coaxing his shepherd to help with the harvest without ever asking him; his presiding presence at the harvest-home feast in the oil-lit barn.

> I can visualize that scene quite clearly: three tables in U-shaped formation, my father in the chair at the top table, and the foreman and myself at the ends of the others. I can see the ruddy countenances of the company, shining like burnished copper in the pool of light from the lamps over-

head. The light would filter through cracks in the reflectors here and there, and faintly outline the arching rafters of the barn, giving the whole scene almost a church-like appearance. Indeed, the company might have been a gathering of old and jolly friars, save that whiskers predominated.

Yet the real message of *Farmer's Glory* is not of the past —nostalgic and beautiful though that past, conjured up out of a boy's memories, was—but of the future, the future of what, in another of his books Street called *Land Everlasting*. For it was written at a time when many despaired of farming, though—thanks to a false economic diagnosis—millions in this and other countries went hungry for lack of the very food their own unemployed labour could have produced. Today, though we are still in the middle of a wonderful technological agricultural revolution that thirty-eight years ago Arthur Street could not have foreseen, we are once more, in deference to an equally false economic diagnosis, pursuing a national policy which every year makes it more difficult for a farmer simultaneously to make a reasonable profit and treat the land itself, the unchanging source of all our agricultural wealth, as it needs to be treated. Though the problem of exporting to other countries on a scale sufficient to pay not only for our essential but our inessential imports is becoming increasingly difficult, nearly half our food is still having to be bought from foreign countries, though our own soil, if our skilful farmers were given the chance, could ultimately feed us. Yet, in spite of the persistent folly of those who rule us and its melancholy consequences, I find in Arthur Street's great book the answer that every farmer has at one time or another in his life to seek and find. "The only real failure in life," he wrote, "is in giving up."

For all those who knew and loved him, this brave, prescient and persistent man lives again in his daughter's, Mrs McCormick's, charming biography. I am proud that she should have asked me, his friend and admirer, to contribute this Foreword to it.

ARTHUR BRYANT

ILLUSTRATIONS

between pages 24 and 25

1 The Street family outside Ditchampton Farm

2 The indispensable Vivi

3, 4 My father and myself, Broad Chalke 1938. With Jorrocks and the milk-float in 1939

5 My father and the film heroine of *Strawberry Roan*

6 The filming of *Strawberry Roan* at Compton Chamberlayne during the war

7 My father on his 1937 Canadian lecture tour with Duncan Marshall, the Canadian Minister of Agriculture

facing page

8 My father and husband with the managing director of Massey Harris at the Bath and West Show, 1949 48

9 My mother, my daughter and myself in 1950 48

10 The tenth birthday edition of "Any Questions" 49

facing page

11 My father doing some early television work with a chicken 49

12 Ditchampton Farm 64

13 My father planning the first improvements to Mill Farm 64

14 In his new study at Mill Farm 65

15 Mill Farm. My mother and father in the drawing-room 80

16 Outside the inn 80

17 Shooting with the ever-faithful Brian in attendance 81

18, 19 A. G. Street the farmer. (*above*) Stooked oats. (*below*) My father always regarded ploughing as the king of jobs 96

20 Fishing at Testwood 97

ACKNOWLEDGEMENTS

The author: 1; 3; 4; 7; 11. *Farmers Weekly*: 2. *Picture Post*: 5; 6; 16. MacLaren Photographs: 8. Camera Press Ltd.: 9. *Hampshire Chronicle*: 10. *Salisbury and Winchester Journal*: 12; 20. John Gay: 13. Associated Newspapers Ltd.: 14; 15; 17. *Daily Mail*: 18. Ford Motor Company Ltd.: 19.

AUTHOR'S NOTE

I wish to express my sincere gratitude to my father's secretary, Beryl Davidge, for her invaluable help and encouragement in the publication of this biography. I should also like to thank Mrs. George Bambridge and Macmillan and Company for permission to quote the lines from Kipling's "The Land" which appear on page 96.

CHAPTER ONE

> **"The only real failure in life is in giving up. On looking back let it stand to our credit in life's balance sheet that at least we tried, and tried hard."**
>
> **A.G.S. *Farmer's Glory***

'A.G.' he was called, even in the hospital where he lay dying. The Sister used to come into his room and say, "Now A.G., you're going to walk out of here on your own two feet." It hardly seemed likely to me, considering the overwhelming odds he was now up against, and I doubt whether she really thought it possible either, but he fought on right to the end.

He had always been a fighter, my father. Life had never been easy for him from the very beginning. He was born with his feet facing the wrong way, and he never walked until he was 7 years old, when he took his first few tottering steps towards the specialist who was rustling a box of chocolates enticingly in front of him. Whilst he was still a baby, he had to have more than one operation before his feet were even pointing the right way, and throughout most of his childhood his legs were encased in irons.

My father was the youngest but one in a family of six.

Being so immobile in his early days, he was forced to struggle and shout in order to get what he wanted or to make his presence felt. Perhaps that was where it all started. He made himself heard all right, especially after he was 40, but the splendid thing about it all was the fact that he always had something interesting to say. I never remember him saying a dull or boring thing in his life. He used to cut through any pretence and get to the heart of a matter in about one sentence. He was the most completely honest man I have ever known. People have called him arrogant, insular, prejudiced and selfish; but he was also kind, lovable, loyal and, above all things, honest. He was always honest with himself, too, which is more than can be said for most of us.

I was sometimes rather afraid of him when I was young. He was so tall, and he was apt to explode at times. I was never quite sure what made him especially upset, except, perhaps, when it rained during haymaking. It was best to keep out of his way then; he used to pace up and down, and my mother said he was like a troubled sea.

Rain was therefore something I loathed, especially during the summer. When my mother once tried to console me while a June downpour was ruining our hay, by saying that God had decided it was necessary to make her flowers grow, she received the doubtful reply, "Yes, perhaps, but I think God's away on holiday just now and some ordinary man is doing His job." It seemed obvious to me that haymaking was infinitely more important than gardening, as any God, if He were on the spot, would surely realize and switch on some sunshine to ease my father's worries.

Soon after I was born in 1921, farming started going downhill fast, so my father must have had good reason to be troubled. He must have had a "lot on his collar", as he used to put it, especially as my mother became very seriously ill at the same time. We nearly went bankrupt but he pulled us through. He was the type who would.

The first time I was made dimly aware of the situation was the Christmas of 1928. I was 7 years old then and my father gave me a very cheap edition of *Hans Andersen's Fairy Tales*. Wretch that I was, I remember being disappointed with it because it contained no really good coloured pictures and the print was so small. He had always been generous about presents and I think this one puzzled me, even at that early age.

Then later on, we did not own a car like the parents of the other children I knew in the little town of Wilton, in Wiltshire, where we lived; instead, we had a large van with A. G. STREET, OPEN-AIR MILK written on its sides. In order to save us from complete bankruptcy, my father had changed his whole system of farming, and now, besides getting up at four thirty a.m. seven days a week to milk seventy cows in an open-air milking outfit, with only the help of one pupil, he also started a milk round in Salisbury, putting on a white coat and doing the delivering himself straight after the morning's milking.

How my father was able to manage all this I simply do not know, except that he always had the most enormous capacity for hard work. He worked all day and every day non-stop, and on Saturdays he would sit at his desk and work far into the night, totting up figures in the milk-books; then he would stump up to bed for a few hours' sleep, before the Sunday morning round-up of the cows (the ladies who paid the rent) started the week rolling all over again.

My father gave up all his recreational activities during those difficult years. He had enjoyed hunting, shooting, fishing, tennis and golf during the prosperous period just after the First World War. Now, all that came to an end. He resigned from every club, and he simply worked.

Just occasionally he must have taken some time off, because there was a never-to-be-forgotten afternoon when he took me to Salisbury and marched me up the steps of what seemed like some palace. Even the new shoes I was wearing seemed to be squeaking in excitement as, in fear and wonder, I climbed higher and higher beside him in this amazing building until we came into a great darkness and fumbled our way into some seats and solemnly sat down.

My father never told me where we were going or that I was in what was known as the 'Picture House'. I doubt I would have been any the wiser if he had. When the screen lit up and a spotted dog came bouncing on to it, my joy knew no bounds. When, a little later, a policeman could be seen chasing the dog before being compelled to stop because his trousers were falling down, I understand I embarrassed my father by standing up and cheering. Nowadays, that place is no longer a cinema; it has been renovated to become the local Arts Theatre, but no production, however good, not even a play of my father's which was once staged there, can equal that wonderful afternoon's entertainment when he first introduced me to the silent screen.

In the winter of 1929 my father caught influenza. He had a tough constitution, but this particular bout laid him really low. He was probably not helped by the fact that the day before he went down with it he took a little more time off in order to run behind me and the bicycle that he was teaching me to ride.

My father was forced to remain indoors for at least a fortnight, an unprecedented thing for him and one which must have worried and irked him unbearably. He became exceptionally provoked one day by reading an article on farming in the *Daily Mail*. My mother challenged him to write a better one, and, because he had nothing else to do, he sat down with the stub of a pencil and did so. When he finished it, he gave it to my mother, who said that, if he crossed out all the swear words, she thought it was not a bad effort. With surprising docility, considering his feelings at the time, my father acted on her advice.

I suppose he must then have got it typed somewhere, because in those days a typewriter was an unheard of thing in our household. In fact, my father rarely wrote anything at all. He loathed writing letters. He must have written the minimum amount of business ones, but the job of writing those of a more personal kind, such as to his relations at Christmas, fell to my mother.

The *Daily Mail* accepted my father's article, published it and paid him three guineas. It must have seemed like a miracle to him. I think he felt that to sit down with a bit of pencil and paper and earn that amount of money in the short space of one hour, without any outlay of physical energy or capital, was practically immoral.

However, having tasted blood, he continued to write, not just articles about farming, but anything and everything. I remember one or two which captured my imagination as a child. There was an article entitled "My Old Blue Suit", which was published with illustrations. I forget the gist of it, and I forget the name of the magazine where it was printed, but I shall never forget the drawing the artist did of my father in his old blue suit, looking rather foolish at some party; it upset me considerably as it did not look like him at all.

The only other thing I can remember him writing in those days was a short story about someone deciphering a code which was written on a very old typewriter such as the one he had now bought himself. I cannot remember whether this story ever did get published because, like all struggling writers, there were plenty of rejection slips, but I know I personally found it as exciting as one by Angela Brazil, whose school adventure books I used to devour regularly.

In the autumn of 1930 I was sent as a day-girl to a good public school in the neighbourhood. It must have been difficult for my father to afford even day fees at the time, but his single-mindedness of purpose was gradually paying off, in spite of the fact that there was, as yet, no sign of any lessening, but more of an intensification of the general farming depression.

My father wanted me to have the best education possible. He came from a family that believed in this. His eldest sister, my Aunt Fanny, was an ardent and fearsome educationalist, finally becoming Acting Principal of Royal Holloway College, which is part of London University and stands, in all its solid forbidding magnificence, beside the main road at Englefield Green. I was horrified to discover that she held high hopes of my going there one day, and regarded it ever afterwards as "the place where Aunt Fanny wanted to shut me up".

My father's four sisters and one brother had all been endowed with good brains by my Grandmother and Grandfather Street. It was, however, strange that it seemed to be the distaff side of the family who remained longest at school and went on to colleges, whilst the boys' formal education ended somewhat abruptly. My father was 15 when he came home from boarding-school for the last time and started working for his father at Ditchampton Farm, on the outskirts of Wilton.

But it was inevitable that a young man of his ability and temperament would soon want more independence, and when he was 18 he quarrelled with his father. In order to prove to both him and himself that he was capable of earning his own living, he went off to Canada and became a hired hand on a farm in the Middle West. As soon as the First World War broke out, he tried to enlist, first in Canada and again on his return to England, where he hoped the Yeomanry might take him, but, to his great annoyance and astonishment, he was rejected both times on the grounds of his bad feet. By this time, the quarrel with his father was long forgotten, and, because the latter was now getting on in years and becoming increasingly crippled by arthritis, there was a ready-made job for my father at home.

My grandfather died in 1917, long before I came on the scene, but I well remember my grandmother, a large Victorian lady with a very definite 'presence'. After my grandfather's death, my father took over the tenancy of Ditchampton Farm at a greatly increased rental and bought the stock and implements with money borrowed from his mother, on which he paid interest.

In 1918 my father married the youngest daughter of the manager of the local felt mills. Wilton, apart from being a carpet town, was, and still is, one of the few places in the country where felt is manufactured. My parents were very much in love, but I understand my mother, who knew nothing of farming life, was rather awed at having to step into the shoes of such a formidable lady as Grandmother Street, who now went off to live with her only unmarried daughter. Whenever she came to visit my parents, she seemed unable to forget that she was no longer the mistress of Ditchampton Farm and was apt to continue giving orders, until my father, with the great tact and diplomacy of which he alone was capable, managed to persuade his mother that, although his wife was young and had not his mother's experience behind her, it was, after all, now her home and she was making a good job of looking after it. To have performed this delicate piece of strategy without a rift in family relations seems to me to have been a stroke of genius.

During my childhood my grandmother came regularly once a week to spend a day with us. She brought her sewing materials and her favourite newspaper. I would sit beside her with a dictionary and help her to do the crossword puzzle. Looking back, I think she probably asked me to look up more words than were strictly necessary because she thought it was good for me.

I know my father worried about the fact that when I first went to public school he was also selling milk to the various house-mistresses in charge there. There was one house-mistress, of whom I was particularly fond because she taught me English, a subject I always enjoyed. My father had to go and ask her for her custom one day, something he dreaded doing. However, the visit went very well. I imagine they soon settled the milk question and got on to more interesting topics. She must have found him an unusual milk retailer, but little did she know that in a few years' time she would be coaching girls for School Certifi-

The Street family outside Ditchampton Farm. My grandfather holding my father, and my Aunt Fanny extreme right.

The indispensable Vivi.

(*above left*) My father and myself, Broad Chalke 1938.
(*above right*) With Jorrocks and the milk-float in 1939.

My father and the film heroine of *Strawberry Roan*.

The filming of *Strawberry Roan* at Compton Chamberlayne during the war.

My father on his 1937 Canadian lecture tour with Duncan Marshall, the Canadian Minister of Agriculture.

cate on a book called *Farmer's Glory*, chosen by the Cambridge Examining Board, which this selfsame man had written.

Although my father's financial position was a little easier now, we were still pretty hard up. I know this because of a gymnastic lesson at school. We were being taught to climb ropes. One day, when I had achieved what I thought was a splendid feat, had reached the very top and was clinging on desperately, waiting to be told to come down, the mistress asked the other girls what was wrong with me. I imagined it had something to do with my grip or my position, and I waited in agony whilst everyone clustered round beneath me, and one bright voice piped up that my "smiles" were my trouble. 'Smiles' in those days were the gaps of flesh we showed between the tops of our stockings and the bottoms of our knickers. I went home mortified, hoping my mother would buy me some longer stockings, but she simply sewed some black material round the tops, because they were new ones and not to be wasted. I often think of this incident now, when I see how the advent of tights beneath the mini-skirt has solved the problem of 'smiles'.

I never knew at the time that my father had started writing a book. I never saw him at it, but that was because he wrote in bed at night at the end of his ordinary working day. I was probably at school when Edith Olivier, the novelist, who lived in Wilton Park and who enjoyed reading his articles, descended on both my parents and in her delightfully imperious way, danced into the room saying, "Arthur, you must write a book. I insist." It was not until a long time afterwards that I heard about all the encouragement my father received from both Edith Olivier and a publishing friend of hers, Mr. Richard de la Mare, who read the manuscript with great enthusiasm.

When *Farmer's Glory* first appeared in 1932, it hit the literary world with a tremendous force. My father was hailed as a second Cobbett. Although he must have been enormously pleased, he was disarmingly modest about it, saying everything about the book had been lucky from the start. He now gave credit where he felt credit was due, not only to Edith Olivier and Richard de la Mare, but also to my mother for never failing to believe in the ultimate outcome. My father also confided in me that much of the material in *Farmer's Glory* had already been sent to Fleet Street in shortened versions and rejected, so that he was a little chary ever afterwards of all the pundits who reigned there.

It must have appealed to his great sense of humour, however, to wake up one morning and read in the papers that he had "the sensuous appreciation of a poet" ("Strewth!"), that his book was a "literary miracle" ("Good Lord!"), and that he "shared with Siegfried Sassoon the gift of evoking the scent of English earth" ("Wonders will never cease!").

CHAPTER TWO

"Tell me, Mr. Street, do you ever sing in your bath?"
A.G.S. in *Wessex Wins* referring to his initiation into the art of broadcasting, 1932.

The immediate success of *Farmer's Glory* did not impress me at the time. With the self-centredness of youth, I was more preoccupied with getting into the netball team in my form. On the top of the bus going to school one day, I was surprised to hear our doctor's eldest daughter saying my father would now be famous. The thought had never occurred to me, but I could see that interesting developments might possibly take place.

At home my father seemed just the same, except that it gradually began to dawn on me that he was away rather a lot. Also, he seemed to be better dressed. By that, I do not mean that he had ever looked untidy or unkempt, but obviously one does not wear the same clothes to milk seventy cows as one would to travel up to the B.B.C. in London and give a broadcast talk, which he often seemed to be doing.

He still got up early and helped with the morning's

milking, but at least once a week and sometimes more often, he would hurry home, have breakfast and change, and catch the London train. He had a foreman on the farm now, who used to drive him to Salisbury station, and one morning they were too late. I was enthralled to hear how Charlie Noble had put his foot down on the accelerator and raced the train to Andover, where they caught up with it and all was well. My father would never let anyone down, especially the B.B.C., and later that morning he was on the air as usual. He had a good broadcasting voice, and his talks about the countryside were greatly enjoyed, both in this country and abroad, particularly by blind or elderly listeners, who sent him a large fan-mail.

My father worried very much about writing a second book, because he said everyone had one book in them but that it took a real author to be able to get two published. However, his fears were groundless. *Strawberry Roan,* a novel which had a calf for its heroine, came out the same year as *Farmer's Glory* and proved to be a great success also. In fact, it was the only one of my father's books that was ever filmed, and, since he had given me the film rights of several of his books, with *Strawberry Roan* amongst them, it was a particularly lucky one for me.

When the actual filming took place, the film unit came down to Wiltshire and shot many of the scenes locally. I used to hang around, hoping they might need an extra, but, as a lanky untidy young girl did not appear to be on their list of requirements, I contented myself with remaining fascinated by all the queer types, especially the cameramen with beards, who pranced about and must have badly shocked the inhabitants of the little villages of Wishford and Compton Chamberlayne.

During those successful and exciting years between the publication of *Farmer's Glory* in 1932 and the outbreak of the Second World War, my father must have done a prodigious amount of work. Books about the countryside, both novels and other kinds, seemed to roll out of his typewriter one after another. Thanks to Frank Morley, a good publishing friend, he became a member of the Savage Club. As a child, I was intrigued and mystified when I once overheard Mr. Morley telling my mother that my father was, like every genius, really two people rolled into one.

It now seemed incredible that this unusual father of mine was playing bridge with Mark Hamburg, A. P. Herbert, and Benno Moiseiwitsch, by whom he was affectionately know as 'Farmer'. Reginald Arkell, who wrote the lyrics for the musical, *1066 and All That*, became a great friend of his, and I gleaned information about people like Flotsam and Jetsam, or Ravenhill, the well-known Punch cartoonist. The latter, knowing I was keen on drawing, sometimes used to write to me, signing himself 'Uncle Raven'. In one of his letters, which I still have, he ends, "All good wishes to your dear mother and that great big lovable man, your father."

Sometimes some of these Savages came to visit us. My mother was once somewhat taken aback when she heard she had to provide lunch for the entire Hamburg family at hardly any notice. Someone was despatched hastily to Salisbury to buy a whole Wiltshire ham, and later that morning the Hamburgs descended on us, complete with pet bulldog. My mother must have risen to the occasion well, because sometime afterwards, when Mark Hamburg met my father in the Savage Club, he said, "Dear boy, the memory of that meal. It is with me now."

But with all this new exciting life, my father never forgot his old friends. He never became grand. Although his life in London and his life in the country were worlds apart, he seemed to be able to integrate the two. He would be just as interested and interesting talking farming with his neighbours as he would be playing bridge or carrying on some ribald conversation into the small hours with brother Savages. Like all loyal people, he always had plenty of friends.

If he had had to give up one life or the other, I know he would have given up his London one. The country always came first. Land was a thing he cared passionately about, as can be witnessed by his remarks in the foreword of one of his books, *In His Own Country*. He says, "It is queer how love for the land, especially love for a farm, gets hold of a man. In most cases, certainly in mine, it transcends all other loves." He also had a very favourite quotation from the Bible, the one which says, "Where your treasure is, there will your heart be also." There was no doubt where his heart lay.

Looking back on those days from my own personal point of view, I much preferred the very rare ones when my father was neither farming nor writing. As he was such a busy man, the times which stand out are those when he was just being a father. Although, as I have said, there were occasions when his temper got the better of him, there were also times when he could be extraordinarily kind and gentle. Soon after I started school I became ill, and our local doctor thought there was something the matter with my heart. I had to stay in bed for a month. Actually, there was nothing much the matter with me at all, but, until I was seen by a London specialist, my father did everything he could to cheer me up.

He used to take time off in order to read to me each day, and the book he chose was *Helen's Babies* by John Habberton, published by Grant Richards in 1899. The tattered remains are in the top of one of my cupboards to this day. On the fly-leaf is an inscription to my grandmother, which reads, "To Mrs. Street's babies with love and good wishes for their welfare from their master and friend, J. Coates, 1.1.1901."

John Coates was the schoolmaster in a little private school in Wilton, a man whom I believe had no little trouble with my father before the latter went on to Dauntsey's School near Devizes. The book he gave to the Street family would probably be considered sentimental rubbish now, but I loved it, especially one of the naughtier characters in it, a little boy called Toddie. There was no end to the dreadful escapades he got up to, and I particularly liked the one where he became ill through drinking a whole bottle of something called 'Paregoric' and had to be tucked under his uncle's arm and rushed to the apothecary's on horseback to be given an emetic.

The other thing I remember when I was ill was that my father always used to buy me nectarines or peaches whenever he went to Salisbury. This kind of fruit seemed to have such an aura of luxury and extravagance. When the doctor pronounced me fit enough, my parents booked a first-class carriage and took me to London to see a specialist. They went to no end of trouble, and there was very little wrong. It was the first time I had ever been to London, and, in spite of feeling rather weak through lying around in bed, I enjoyed it all tremendously.

The other days when I remember my father very clearly are those we spent in the water-meadows. The scent of willowherb and meadow-sweet always evokes a special nostalgia, and I can see him now, rod in hand, casting for trout or grayling on the river Wylye. He was very tall and quite thin in those days. He always walked with a slight limp, due to the disability he suffered as a child, but this made no difference to the distance he could cover.

It was always a great grief to my father that he was rejected by the army as soon as the doctors discovered his mis-shapen feet. He could not believe that they would not accept him, in the Yeomanry at least. In vain, he told the authorities that he had walked twenty miles on snow shoes in Canada. He had become so used to putting up with his handicap, it came as a great shock that anyone should take it so seriously. He never let it interfere with his life, though, perhaps, it made him self-conscious in public, especially as a young man. He therefore had a very understandable desire for privacy and a very real loathing of large crowds. My mother had a great deal to do with helping him overcome this, for which he was always very grateful.

My father was a very keen fisherman, but when I was young the most fishing he ever got was the odd day or two each year on the river Wylye, given to him by the club which had the rights of the water running through our farm, or rather the farm which my father rented from the Earl of Pembroke. On these occasions it was my job to hold the net and keep either very close behind him or a good way away so that I did not get hooked myself when he was casting.

Sometimes we took our lunch with us; occasionally we had it at an inn. When he caught a fish, and I happened to be lagging far behind thinking about something else, there was an almighty bellow, and I had to double up to help with the landing. On good days, on the way home, we often stopped to leave some trout with his various friends and neighbours.

In this very same river my father also taught me to swim. It was fairly weedy, but there were certain places where it was considered safe and possible. After I became proficient, he used to take me to some deeper water running beneath a railway bridge which we called the Black Arch. There was something vaguely exciting and sinister about the name, and it gave me immense satisfaction to be thought capable of disporting myself there.

Usually we had one or two other children with us, either cousins or friends of mine. My father was always very good with young people. He studied them and took a great interest in them, and they all loved him. When he died, I had letters from friends of my youth with whom I had lost touch, saying how they remembered all the happy days they had spent at Ditchampton Farm where I was brought up. For a man who was quick-witted and did not suffer fools gladly, he was extraordinarily patient with the young, taking no end of trouble to explain things to them.

He once spent hours helping a young nephew to make a wireless set. They would buy valves and wire and goodness knows what, and great was the jubilation when the Savoy Orpheans first crackled through. He also took a great liking to one of our doctor's sons, with whose sisters I went to school. This particular one he used to call a "most attractive scallywag". I cannot remember Tommy ever doing any work in his youth, but he became a fully-fledged doctor in the course of time. During my father's last illness, although Tommy was now a busy G.P. living some distance away, he often managed to find time to visit him in hospital. These purely social calls meant a great deal to the patient who was once responsible for teaching his visitor some of the finer points connected with country sport.

Another friend of mine, a girl who used to live near us, said to me not long ago, "You know, he had such a magnetic personality, your father. If he had ever asked me to do something extraordinary like suddenly dressing up and doing a dance in Salisbury market-square, I should have obeyed him without question. Yes, without question."

During most of my childhood, we had farm pupils living in our house. In the beginning, this was mostly for economic reasons on our side, but the pupils got a good bargain too. Later on, when my father's literary work took him away from home so much, he gave up having them, and I know he also thought it was time my mother had a rest from catering for such hefty youths. Our household reverted to its normal size, which consisted of my mother and father, myself, and a most remarkable cousin of mine called Vivi.

Vivi had come to live with us when I was born. She was then about 16 years old and had come to help with 'the baby'. In a very short space of time she became indispensable because my mother was so ill. Vivi did everything. She cooked and cleaned, nursed my mother, looked after me, tended all our various domestic pets and, with maturity, gave orders to my father. Without Vivi, I cannot imagine what would have happened to us all. She died just fifteen months after my father, and the world seems a lesser place now that they have gone.

CHAPTER THREE

"Let me get my rural status clearly defined; I am merely a humble tenant farmer in the county of Wiltshire."

A.G.S. *Ditchampton Farm*

"I was speaking as a barrister with a brief, a brief for the Wheat Quota. You were speaking from the heart. That always wins, even against the expert."

Sir Ernest Shepperton to A.G.S. after their lectures at Ashridge, the Bonar Law College, in 1932.

In 1934 my father did a thrilling thing. He bought me a pony. He told me afterwards that he would have done so before, if he had known how much I wanted one. I think I had an idea that ponies were fabulously expensive; the years when we were hard up had made an impression on me, so that I never told anyone how keen I was to ride.

However, my eyes came to my aid over this because the oculist regarded my progressive short-sight as a serious matter which might be arrested if I did no school work for a term, at least. Nowadays, such old-fashioned notions would be frowned upon, but when I was 13 to have a whole summer away from school seemed like an order from the most sensible physician in the world.

Practical as always, my father immediately thought about what I was going to do with myself. To have an only child aged 13 "lopping around", as he put it, without any definite purpose for such an indefinite time, was asking for trouble. If I was not to be allowed to use my eyes on any close work, I would obviously have to be out of doors, and a pony seemed the ideal answer.

Knowing that this idea met with such approval, he was carried away by enthusiasm. I think his optimistic and enthusiastic approach to any problem was one of the most endearing things about my father, something which he kept right until his death. Even when he was so paralysed by his last illness, his enthusiasm for life still shone forth whilst he described to me, in absolute detail, the sort of apparatus which would enable him to become independent again when he came out of hospital, and which he wanted me to get made.

But, back in 1934, my father had only to tell his various friends that he was on the look-out for a suitable pony for me, and soon, the rural grapevine, that never-failing means of communication, brought satisfactory results. An old cattle-dealer by the name of Spiller, who lived some six miles away, rode over to see my father and told him he had "just the job" for a beginner. Spiller was a bit of a rough diamond, but in all our dealings with him he was more of a gentleman than many people who like to think of themselves as such. My father and Spiller had a mutual trust in each other, a kind of intangible relationship which defies description and would possibly be spoilt by any attempt on my part to do so. With true countryfolk there always seem to be these certain unwritten rules of behaviour which have been handed down throughout the generations and continue, not by any verbal instructions, but by some innate good sense of what is right and proper.

"Just the job" turned out to be a rather rough-coated brown pony called Toby of about thirteen hands. Spiller assured us that he neither kicked, bucked, reared, nor bolted for home, but that there was plenty of life in him. He said, in fact, he had let "our Mavis", his own grand-daughter, ride him. That clinched the deal, and soon Toby was installed in one of the loose-boxes at Ditchampton Farm.

During that summer I virtually lived with Toby, except when hunger and Vivi's calls brought me into the house or nightfall necessitated a few hours parting. My father and Spiller taught me to ride Toby and to look after him. There was a field by our house which was known as 'the Park'. It sounded rather grand, but it only consisted of a small triangular-shaped piece of ground with a good slope where I first kicked Toby into a canter pointing away from home, whilst my father (so I learned afterwards) held his breath at the gate.

I suppose the idea must have already occurred to him, because he was a man whose mind was always several jumps ahead of everyone else's, but, sooner rather than later, the problem of where I could ride further afield arose. In a very short space of time Toby and I had outgrown the Park, and, with all Spiller's numerous occupations, he could hardly be expected to keep coming to our house to take me for a ride. I was not proficient enough to be allowed to go alone, so my father, probably having waited just long enough to see how I took to riding, bought himself a horse, and we sallied forth together.

I do not suppose he ever thought he would ride again after he had given it up in the early nineteen twenties. He had now passed his forty-third birthday, and was beginning to put on weight, but he felt, to use one of his well-known Wiltshire expressions, "force put". I think it must have been extremely disheartening for him, however, to be told by a critical daughter when he first came down to breakfast in his new jodhpurs that his "bottom half looked too young". Youth is very thoughtless.

Other than this, I do not know what his feelings were about taking up riding once more. I think it is quite likely that he did not want to bother with it at all, but I do know that, after a little while, it gave him the most enormous pleasure. He even became secretary of the local hunt, and riding assumed a very important place in both our lives.

I got to know my father very well in those years. We used to ride together whenever it was possible, although he was often away in different parts of the country on lecture tours. When this happened, he always telephoned my mother to say where he was staying each night. Sometimes calls came from the remotest parts of Scotland; sometimes from the industrial Midlands, where members of various luncheon clubs were very keen on his lectures; sometimes from Wales; sometimes from university towns or places like Ashridge, the Bonar Law College, where he was often asked to speak on agriculture.

Sometimes my mother accompanied him on his tours, and just occasionally I was able to go also. On one occasion we all stayed in Harrogate with the mother of Winifred Holtby, the author of *South Riding*. It was just after Winifred Holtby died, and Mrs. Holtby laid great emphasis on the fact that I was to occupy her daughter's one-time bedroom. Being a somewhat imaginative young girl, I did not care for the idea at all. I was more than a little afraid of Mrs.

Holtby, who was a very imposing old lady and reminded me of my Grandmother Street. After dinner on the first night of our visit, she wound up some long story she was telling us by suddenly directing her gaze towards the corner where I was sitting, stifling a yawn and saying, "And now, my dear, you *may* go to bed." I obeyed immediately, although secretly hoping to have been ignored until we could all go upstairs together.

But always, as my father's tours drew to an end and his car was pointing towards Wiltshire again, it seemed as though he was chafing at the bit and longing to get home. He deplored fast driving, but he tried to organize himself so that he spent the least number of nights away. He never enjoyed holidays either, and, as he grew older, he hated sleeping out of his own bed.

I remember once expecting him back at midday, but receiving a call from Oxford the previous evening. "I'll be back by eleven tonight," he said, and then, as soon as he got inside the front door, "just let me get at my desk." He would then quickly go through his mail, because "Tomorrow morning, first thing, I must straighten out my life." Unanswered letters or unpaid bills were anathema to him, and, if ever he was away more than a day or two, any correspondent would receive a letter from his secretary, stating the position and saying that his or her letter would be attended to immediately on Mr. Street's return. That way he reckoned people knew where they were.

It always infuriated him if someone promised to write or telephone him on a certain day and then failed to do so. "Gross inefficiency," he would growl, throwing his pencil across his desk. He himself never let anybody down. If a certain article he had written had to be in a certain office in Fleet Street at a certain time on a certain day, then it would be there, even if he had to deliver it personally. He was utterly reliable in this, so that when he became really ill for the last time, it was pathetic to witness his once-active brain worrying and struggling to write his usual article for the *Farmers Weekly* in order to reach the editor by the first post on Tuesday morning, something which, until then had happened without fail every week for over thirty years.

I suppose back in 1934 my father must have written something in the Press about taking up riding again, because this soon brought the most amazing results. An elderly lady called Miss Darbyshire suddenly wrote to my father and asked him if he would accept her two aged hunters, as she could ride no more and wanted to find good homes for them. My father's writings must have appealed to her, and I suppose she knew that 'Peter' and 'Sea of Glory' would end their days happily if they came to Ditchampton Farm. She so obviously wanted this to take place that, in the end, my father accepted her generous offer on the strict understanding that the horses would be with us until they died.

Peter was a wonderfully safe mount for my father, a "real gentleman" as he put it. Sea of Glory was a more flighty creature, a most beautiful chestnut mare. Like most women, if she got at all upset, she would 'carry on' a bit and a slightly wild look would come into her eyes, although on the whole she was a very sweet animal and much admired. We bred from her, and her colt was born at four a.m. one morning when my mother and father returned from the local hunt ball. We had acquired a groom-gardener by then, and Hibberd had been sitting up with her all night. My mother and father arrived in time for the birth, and I was desolated not to have been there also. With a mother whose name was Sea of Glory now owned by a man who had written *Farmer's Glory*, it was fairly obvious what the colt would be called. My father gave him to me, and I hastened to write and tell Miss Darbyshire such wonderful news. Ever since her hunters had come to us, I had written to her regularly with detailed progress reports on them both, and I think this latest event must have made her very happy.

I thought about little else except horses in those years. I joined the local Pony Club and went to all the rallies, and my father arranged for me to have some rather special tuition from a slightly more qualified instructor than Spiller. Instead of the latter's vociferous, "Thee do want to grip with thy knees, zno", I was a little hurt to receive orders to lengthen my stirrups and spend whole afternoons jogging round in a circle in order to improve my 'seat'.

CHAPTER FOUR

> "When I pick up my Sunday paper and see in large headlines that Mr. So-and-So has written a brilliantly clever book, I always say to myself, 'Ah well, Stanley, we can afford to give that one a miss'. Now you listen to me for a moment, young man. You go home and write another book, and whatever you do, don't try to be clever."
>
> A.G.S. in *Wessex Wins* referring to a meeting with Stanley Baldwin in 1932.

I started keeping a five-year diary in 1937, and it is on my desk now. I see on the front I have drawn pictures of the five horses which inhabited our stables during all or part of that year, namely: Peter, Sea of Glory, Farmer's Glory, Tommy and Black Bess. By this time my legs had grown very long, and Toby had to be replaced, first by a rather lazy unsatisfactory cob called Tommy and then by a livelier animal called Black Bess.

Parting from Toby was agony. I had loved him passionately and cared for him so that the rough coat he arrived with was transformed by clipping and grooming into something which shone in the sunlight. I used to smooth and burnish him with curry comb and body brush, and not once or twice, but thrice a day, I would clean out his hooves with the old-fashioned hoof-pick with which I had been presented by our local blacksmith.

Toby had never let me down, and the only serious fall which occurred whilst riding him was through my own stupidity and conceit. I had been taken to the circus and became fascinated by the feats of the bareback riders. The next morning I took Toby into the Park and attempted to do likewise. He put up with all my experiments patiently, and I was quite pleased with our progress, so pleased, in fact, that triumphantly, I rode him at too smart a trot back to the stables in time for lunch. As I turned him sharply to the right through the gates, he slipped on some cobble-stones and went down heavily. I was thrown in between him and a brick wall, on which I narrowly missed banging my head. My mother and father, hearing the commotion, were over in the stables within seconds, thankful to find Toby and me consoling each other in his box, with nothing the matter with either of us except a few bruises and scratches.

As I watched Hibberd lead Toby down the drive of Ditchampton Farm for the last time on his way to the home of a girl friend of mine, who was younger and shorter than myself, the tears began to roll down my cheeks. My father stood by me until we saw the last little bit of him disappear under the railway arch at the end of the road. Then he turned to me, put his arm on my shoulder and, knowing how I felt, said, "That's as it should be. Now, let's go to the pictures."

Although I had become very keen on hunting by now, it was always a morning's cubbing which appealed to me most. I am rather ashamed to say that at that time I simply never thought about the fox one way or another. It was the riding, the jumping, the early morning mists in the valleys whilst we waited by some huge clump of trees on top of the Wiltshire downs, and the company of my father and the whole fraternity of horsey people that made those days so unforgettable.

When I say "horsey people", I do not mean those with completely one-track minds, who did nothing else but hunt foxes and shout "Tally-ho". I myself was probably more guilty of this than any of the others, but it was the strange mixture of people from all walks of life who enjoyed this common bond, which made it all so attractive. I think the diversity of the field was something which especially appealed to my father. He used to get on so well with everyone. There was still, in those days, one sporting parson; there was a most handsome amateur whipper-in, the son of a retired doctor, to whom I completely lost my heart; sometimes there was Spiller, who would appear from nowhere like some genie, looking benevolent and ferocious at the same time, with his huge moustache and steel-rimmed spectacles; sometimes 'our Mavis' accompanied him on a leading-rein; then there was the odd colonel, the devastatingly glamorous girl who ran the Pony Club, the blacksmith's son and so on.

On cubbing mornings my father would set his alarm and come in and waken me at the appointed time. Then we would both get up, and I would get breakfast whilst he saddled the horses. Early in the season we would sometimes set off in pitch darkness, clattering down through the silent streets of Wilton. We went single file, although at that time and in those days we never met any traffic. I can see the sparks from Peter's hooves now as they struck the tarmac in front of me. Not a soul was about; just occasionally there was a light in an upstairs window, where, perhaps, someone was sitting up with a sick child or an elderly parent. I hope we did not disturb the populace too much as the sound of our horses' hooves rang out in the deserted streets.

I always feared that we would never get to the meet on time. Although it did not matter so much when one was cubbing (and I think my father would often have been quite content to join the hounds later on after they had moved off), it was a point of honour with me that we were in at the beginning and, I used to hope, the end. One morning, for some reason or other, we were a little on the late side starting, so I egged my father on to gallop over the downs in order to get to the 'Black Horse' at Teffont by six-thirty a.m. It was going to be a hot day, one could tell. Our horses started to sweat and, although we slowed up and walked them sedately for the last mile or so, we were still sending up clouds of steam when the Master greeted us, a most disgraceful state of affairs. "What have we here," he asked, adjusting his monocle, "last year's race?" He was very fond of my father, and the joke was all in good fun, but I never asked to gallop to a meet again. A little later on I received a letter from this selfsame Master presenting me with the Wilton Hunt Button, an honour which to me, at that age, was beyond price.

My diary has brought the year 1937 quite sharply back into focus now. I see that on Wednesday, 17th February, Peter died. There is a cut-out of him from an old photograph pasted on to that day's entry, which I have ringed in black. Two days prior to this I read, "Pete no better. Daddy wrote to Miss Darbyshire." This was obviously not the sort of occasion for a letter from me.

A fortnight after this sad episode I see another entry

which reads, "Daddy will go to America in June", followed by seven exclamation marks. Nowadays, when people fly back and forth across the Atlantic and think no more of it than a trip to Scotland, my punctuation seems a little superfluous, but back in 1937, the fact that my father had been asked by Duncan Marshall, the Canadian Minister of Agriculture, to do a lecture tour of the Middle West of both Canada and the States, was an event indeed.

My father sailed from Southampton on the S.S. *Montclair* on 26th May, and we went down to see him off. I wore a new bright pink suit, and in the first letter he wrote to me he remarked that it was a good colour to wear for the occasion, as he could still see me when all else had faded into obscurity. I suppose we must always have been an emotional and rather tender-hearted family. My mother and I stayed till the *Montclair* sailed out of sight, and I read in my diary that the day before this my mother presented my father with a gold pencil and I gave him some cuff-links and a card. I cannot imagine what my cuff-links could have been like or that he was ever able to wear them.

Communication also, has always played a big part in all our lives. The day after he sailed I note that both my mother and I wrote to him, and in my innocence, I entered in my diary, "There is another ship sailing tomorrow," on which, presumably, I thought our letters might travel. Two days later my mother received a letter posted from Cherbourg, and on 4th June a cable came telling us of his safe arrival.

During the time my father was away I struggled with School Certificate, the equivalent to present-day 'O' levels. My father wrote to us regularly, and we wrote back, although there was always a doubt on our part as to whether our letters would ever arrive on time at his various destinations. His letters to me were always full of humour. In one which he wrote from the Ministry's office he says, "I can hear Dunc wrestling with telephone and dictaphone in the next room, and, believe me, if Ontario is wise, she will obey orders. His sec. has just come in to ask me for the last pages of my *Farmers Weekly* article. Early this morning she was glad to know me, now she is proud to type for me. She says she can read my pencilled scrawl. If she can, I am proud to know her." Evidently he was still managing to write articles for the *Farmers Weekly* in the middle of his lecture tour.

Although the whole visit was immensely successful and interesting, I think much of what he saw depressed him. When he got back, I used to hear him talking gravely and at great length about the huge dust bowl in the Middle West and his concern for the places he had revisited, where, nearly a quarter of a century previously, when he was quite a young man, he had been a hired hand, ploughing up virgin soil and proving to himself and his family that he was capable of standing on his own feet.

The day before he returned to this country on the *Empress of Britain*, we received a telephone call from him whilst the ship was still out in the Atlantic. As always, he was like a horse longing to get back to its stable. The pull of England and his home was so great that he had somehow managed to arrange, through various contacts of his, that he would be allowed to get off the boat at ten p.m. the following evening, whilst everyone else had to wait to disembark in the morning. His love of the land which bred him transcended everything, and in another of his letters to me, written from Ontario, he said, "When next anyone

My father and husband (*left*) with the managing director of Massey Harris at the Bath and West Show, 1949.

My mother, my daughter and myself in 1950.

The tenth birthday edition of "Any Questions". *Left to right*: Lord Boothby; Anthony Wedgwood Benn; Baroness Asquith; A. G. Street; Freddie Grisewood; Michael Bowen.

My father doing some early television work with a chicken, although he disliked poultry intensely.

writes enclose lots of snaps, of the house, of you and Mummy and everything to do with our home and English farm life." I suspect that, although everyone over there was clamouring to know how he lived, he had other personal reasons for wanting more photographs.

Hibberd, the groom-gardener, drove my mother and me down to Southampton docks to meet him when he returned. It was the middle of July, and my exams were over. Although it was the summer of 1937, there were obviously some far-sighted people acutely aware of the political situation, because Southampton was having a mock black-out that evening. Hibberd, a conscientious but rather nervous man, had the greatest difficulty in finding the correct dock. In the all-pervading gloom, I remember my father, all alone, bolting down the gangplank, like a large hunter desperately anxious to get out of its horse-box.

It was good to have him home again. He was understandably tired after such a gruelling six weeks, but soon he was farming, writing, broadcasting and lecturing again, weaving all four into that successful pattern of living which, by now, we had all come to take as a matter of course. He was sometimes asked why he never took up politics as well. Certainly, people tried to persuade him; but, although he took a great interest in government and world affairs, he was always too much of a rugged individualist ever to become a party man. He stood alone throughout his life and refused to join a single committee.

In yet another of the letters which he once wrote to me he says, "The great thing is to hang on to one or two principles that one is certain are right, hang on like grim death in the face of superiors if need be, and for the rest, deal with life as it comes . . . the whole art of living is to learn how to do something one loathes . . . life is always uphill, with very occasional glorious downhill bursts . . . you may not like your job at the moment, well, I cannot remember ever liking being a retail milkman." Those words were written to me when I was 22. I am sorry to say that I did not have the wisdom to appreciate them then. I am 47 now. His letter is beside me as I type, and I know how true, how very true they are.

At heart, I think my father was always more of a Liberal than anything else, like his own father was before him, although he once told me that he had voted for all three political parties at different times during his life. At one period, when the late Stanley Baldwin was Lord President of the Council and had come to stay at Wilton House with the Earl and Countess of Pembroke, he asked to meet my father. They had quite a long session together, and I imagine my father, as usual, 'gave it to him straight'. When they parted, Baldwin said, "Remember Mr. Street, we shall be in for the next three or four years, no matter what the other side thinks or does. If we should happen to do one little thing right in agricultural policy, you will send me a post-card, won't you?" My father never found occasion to write one.

I left school at the beginning of 1938, much, I believe now, to my father's disappointment. He had wanted me to try for Oxford, but I had balked at it and inveigled him into promising that, if I passed School Certificate, he would let me leave school and take up art. As he always kept his promises, no pressure was brought to bear, and he did all he could to encourage me in doing what I wanted. I have often regretted my decision and wished that my father could have lived long enough to know that his only grand-daughter, in the face of far greater competition, had gained a place at Somerville.

My efforts at art were sporadic and half-hearted. I still spent a good deal of time riding and hunting, and my days at the local art school were somewhat sandwiched in between. Like many young girls, I hoped vaguely I might get to London in time and attend the Slade School, but the outbreak of war put an end to any such ideas.

I could not imagine a war or believe that one would ever take place, but I know that Mr. Chamberlain's visit to Germany in 1938 thoroughly upset my father. The idea that a British Prime Minister was the one who actually had to do the travelling, with cap in hand, in order to see such a blackguard as Hitler was more than he could take; and when Mr. Chamberlain returned with his 'Peace with Honour' slogan, my father felt ashamed. We may have got 'peace' for a time, at least, but in his eyes there was no 'honour' attached to it. A little later on, when we were cubbing on top of the downs on a particularly beautiful morning, when the mist was just beginning to disperse enough to see the little village of Broad Chalke below us, a rather happy-go-lucky gentleman remarked to my father that it was mornings such as these that ought to make us feel grateful to Mr. Chamberlain. I think my father's reply was more or less unprintable.

However, the uneasy autumn and winter of 1938 passed with my father and myself hunting whenever possible. By now I had learnt to drive a car and consequently had become a great deal more independent. My father had purchased an old Baby Austin in which I used to racket around. Although I had done quite a lot of driving already on our farm, my father arranged for me to be taught professionally by a great friend of his who owned the local garage, and Mr. Moore and I used to drive to the meets when they were too far away to make it practicable to go on horse-back, thereby combining lessons and pleasure. My father was always very keen that I should do things in the same way and at the same time as other girls with whom I had been brought up, but I understand that the first day I took AXY (as we called the car) out by myself after passing my test, aged him considerably.

He was, I suppose, a nervous man, but at the same time a very brave one. He was never afraid to do anything which he thought he should do, however irksome or dangerous; he always said exactly what he thought about everything and never, as it were, 'dodged the issue'. His make-up abounded in those two important ingredients; integrity and plain common sense.

Many people have remarked to me that my father was Churchillian in his attitude to life, and I think this is very true. In his book, *Farmer's Glory,* he writes about his own father saying, "'he had his little ways' . . . but unlike King John, if history tells us true, he had his 'big ways', and they were splendid. In my youth I railed often at the many little things he did, but in every big crisis of my life I never turned to my father in vain. That is, I think, a wholesome memory for any man to leave his son." It is that same memory which the son has left with me, his daughter.

CHAPTER FIVE

"To make land serve man, man must first be content to serve the land."

A.G.S. *Hitler's Whistle*

On 3rd September, 1939, my mother, father, Vivi and I sat in the drawing-room at Ditchampton Farm and listened in silence as Mr. Chamberlain's voice came over the air, telling us we were at war with Germany. In keeping with countless other families all over Britain, there was a sudden and dramatic change in our way of life.

Charlie Noble, our foreman, being a reservist, disappeared virtually overnight; our farmhouse became filled with evacuees from Portsmouth; my father's income looked like immediately being reduced to half or even a quarter of its usual amount, as it seemed that most of his broadcasting and journalistic work would cease. For this reason, by mutual agreement, his secretary left to take a job elsewhere, and I became a glorified untrained land-girl cum secretary in her place. But our lot was nothing compared to families like the Nobles, who were parting with husbands and fathers and sons, or the parents who were saying good-bye to the small children, complete with labels and gas-masks, whom my father and I had collected from Wilton station, and my mother and Vivi had popped into various beds.

My parents had recently altered our house out of all recognition. Although both farm and house were rented, my father decided it was worth having quite extensive alterations done. He wanted a study tucked away somewhere, instead of his present one at the front of the house, where he said he was in full view of anyone arriving at the front door and therefore much too easily 'got at', as he put it. He also wanted the staircase moved, as it annoyed him that it was the first thing one saw on entering the hall and was far from beautiful; and both my mother and father wanted a larger drawing-room, where they could entertain and where I, too, might have small parties if they put down a suitable floor for dancing.

My mother had always been very keen on the house and garden. Over the past few years she had been able to indulge in what my father called her favourite sport of 'sale-ing' and had collected a number of antiques. As my mother was not very strong, and my father was always concerned about her welfare, it sometimes caused consternation when visitors heard him remark cheerfully in her absence, "My wife is sale-ing today," especially if a gale force wind was blowing outside.

I once wrote in my diary, "Mummy and Vivi to a furniture sale—terribly late back so Daddy went to find them." My father hated any of us being late if we had not let him know beforehand. At one time during my youth I was not in from a party when expected. In vain I pleaded that I hoped he might have been asleep and did not want to disturb him; in vain I said, quite truthfully, that the taxi which was to have brought me back failed to arrive; in vain I said that I had been offered a lift by some Americans who seemed to be on the point of leaving every minute for at least two hours. It was to no avail. According to my father I had had neither the "courtesy" nor the "gumption" to telephone, and when he arrived at two a.m. on the doorstep of the house where the party was being held, the wrath that I engendered on the way home was something I remember to this day.

He always said it was the "peasant" in him that made him want to see everyone was in safely at night, a sort of relic from those old patriarchal families, where all the members and all the animals were rounded up at eventide. Although I had just as good a time, and probably better, than any of my girl friends when I was young, I now accepted the fact that if I wanted to go "howling about at night", to use another of his expressions, I was very careful to inform my parents if the 'howling' was going to go on longer than expected. Sometimes, when I think of what goes on with the young at the present day, I do not think it was such a bad idea either.

Just before war broke out, I think both my parents were very pleased with their joint efforts over the improvements to our house. I know I was especially pleased with the drawing-room floor for these dances I hoped to have, and where, presumably, the 'howling about' would be done by my guests. I was also delighted with my bedroom, in which I had been given a free rein with the decorations. As I had been passing through a rather melancholy stage owing to unrequited love, I had chosen mauve walls and grey paintwork, and the whole effect was slightly macabre, but it suited my frame of mind.

But at the beginning of September 1939 I had to stop being the tragedy queen and give over my boudoir to three little girls from Portsmouth until another bedroom could be made ready for them. They were enchanting children, but they had never seen running water in a bedroom before. Quick as a flash, the leader of the gang filled up the basin and splashed gigantic wet murals all over one wall. The next thing we knew was that the mother of one of them arrived at the back door carrying a baby. We were already full up, but my mother and Vivi had not the heart to send her elsewhere, so she lived with us for quite a time and was very useful helping to look after the other children.

Looking back, I think I was probably of more use to the war effort during those first few months than at any other time during the next six years. I was not very efficient either at driving a tractor or typing, but I could do both after a fashion and, possibly more important, exactly when my father required. My mathematics were not a strong point either, but I managed to do the pay for him, which in those days was not the complicated affair it is now.

I remember once my father leaving me chain-harrowing in a field on top of the downs. My eyesight has never been good, and for some reason I found it incredibly difficult to see where I had been and to keep a straight line. Nothing one does in the countryside can ever be secret; one's work is exposed to full view for miles around; sooner or later a farmer on the opposite slope noticed the rather wavering stop-go, stop-go efforts on our side of the valley. It so happened that he had to go into Wilton, met my father and remarked that he must have engaged a new tractor-driver.

My father had not left me long, but he was back in that field within minutes. I rather expected a ticking-off, but he roared with laughter and proceeded to get up on the tractor and give me a few more hints on how to deal with the situation.

Owing to his increasing weight over the last year or so, my father had purchased a heavyweight hunter called Jorrocks. They were rather a splendid pair together in the hunting field. There was something similar in the nature of both man and beast. We now introduced this sensible and willing animal to an old milk-float, which he condescended to pull manfully as his own particular war effort, and he became quite useful on the farm, doing all kinds of jobs, including hauling milk churns. But my father's system of farming was once more being changed, and everywhere grassland was being turned back into arable to feed an island nation in wartime.

In 1939 everybody began boosting British farming. It became the fashionable thing to do, but my father began his campaign in the early nineteen thirties, when he stood alone as its champion. I think it is no exaggeration to say that, during those years preceding the Second World War, he gave British farming more publicity, encouragement and help than any other writer in the country, when to do so was not always popular. He was right about food storage; he was right about grassing down and going in for livestock so that there would be a huge store of fertility under the green turf when war came. He made townsfolk aware that the countryside was not just a playground but their fourth line of defence in time of war and famine, so that when the Battle of the Atlantic came, half of it was fought and won on the fields of Britain. An extract from a poem I wrote at that time for the *Field* perhaps paints the picture a little more colourfully than I can do now:

Poor's Gorse lies still this-morning, and there comes no 'Tally-ho'
From the mist that hangs in patches on the down,
But something in Ten Acre moves already to and fro
And the green is melting slowly into brown.
The sun breaks through the grey sky and the strips of dark earth meet,
Jorrocks plods on steadily—ploughing up for wheat.

We no longer rode or hunted. Sea of Glory had died by now; Farmer's Glory we turned out to grass in the Park, still unbroken. I had a good little thoroughbred hunter at that time, but we sold him, and my regrets were no longer like those when I watched Toby disappear. If the truth be known, I was beginning to lose my nerve, and riding ceased to become such an attraction. Other things had taken its place, and, although just occasionally, even now, I still wonder what it would be like to clamber upon a horse again and turn it towards a jump, I know my courage would fail me, and I am not the carefree and possibly foolhardy equestrienne that I was during those years just before the war.

After the initial upheaval in our lives, gradually things came back to normal, or at least as normal as they could be in wartime. As no bombers appeared over Portsmouth, our evacuees trickled slowly back there again. The Southern Command took over Wilton House, and we had officers billeted on us instead of children. Being a key agricultural worker, Charlie Noble was released from the army and returned to Ditchampton Farm, whilst it appeared that my father would still be wanted as a journalist and broadcaster.

I, myself, became restless. With Charlie once more my father's right-hand man, there was now not so much need for me to run errands and try and hold the fort in his absence. Although, with a return to arable farming, it was obvious more labour would be required, and I could perfectly well have spent the whole war working at home, it somehow did not seem to me to be a proper job. I could take a day off whenever I wanted one. I could lie in bed in the mornings whenever I had been out late. To be really in on the war, it seemed to me that I ought to leave home and get myself into uniform of some sort. When Dunkirk came, in between haymaking I helped at a canteen on Salisbury station. After I had seen the thousands of weary troops who passed through I could wait no longer, and soon afterwards got a job as a V.A.D. in the local hospital.

I think my father also chafed that he could not take a more active part in the war. It always upset him that he had been rejected for the army in 1914 because of his lameness. Knowing his passionate love of England, I think it hurt him more than most that he was prevented from fighting for her. When he heard the appeal over the radio for Local Defence Volunteers, he was up and out of the room and round at Wilton Police Station to put his name down before anyone else arrived. He subsequently became an officer in the Home Guard, taking his responsibilities very seriously.

Sometimes he was asked to lecture to the troops, and he went down well with them. He always had a most attractive sense of humour and a fund of good stories, and I think they probably sensed, even when he was simply talking about agriculture, that here was a man with a fighting spirit.

It was not until the winter of 1943 that I had any reason to be concerned about my father's health. He had always been such a tower of strength, one could not imagine him being ill, at least, not for very long. For my sins, I had now changed jobs again, not this time entirely on my own volition, but it became apparent that both physically and mentally I was not cut out to stand up to any long hours of nursing.

After a period in the ranks, I had now become an officer in the A.T.S. Through letters from home, I gathered that my father was not well, but I had no idea of the seriousness of his condition. He had been sent to Ruthin Castle in North Wales in order, so he wrote cheerfully, to reduce his weight. He said I was not to worry and that he was having the best holiday in his life; also that he had been nicknamed 'Uncle Arthur of the South Wing'.

He came home in time for Christmas, and I got back on leave soon afterwards. When I walked into the drawing-room and saw him sitting on the sofa, I was scared. He seemed to have shrunk out of all recognition but he was as cheerful as ever. My mother and Vivi had gone down with influenza, so I did what I could towards the usual household chores and tried to produce a few meals for us all. They were not very well cooked, and I can remember my father and myself sitting down to a rather poor supper together. When I apologized for it he said, "Never mind. As long as we see to the essentials and get the invalids fed, you and I can do without the frills."

It was not until a long time afterwards, when the war had been over some time, that I learned he had been told that he had a bad heart and, if he did not obey the specialist's orders absolutely, he might only have six months to live. That very same specialist died himself quite a number of years before my father, who was then topping sixteen stone again. When he read about it in the newspapers, my father poured himself a large whisky and soda and shook his head. "Doctors," he remarked, "they're all the same. They don't really know very much. That's why they're all *practising*, you see."

CHAPTER SIX

> "It is good fortune for any man to be able to farm a patch of his native land, especially when that happens to be a patch of Britain."
>
> A.G.S. *Master of None*

I married just after the end of the war, to be precise on 3rd July, 1945, a date which happened to be my husband's birthday and my mother and father's own wedding day, way back in 1918. It seemed strange to be leaving Ditchampton Farm, the home I had known since babyhood, and embarking on a whole new way of life. Just a few days before our wedding, my father fell down in the haymaking field and hurt his shoulder. It was thought that possibly his fall might have had something to do with his heart, and the doctor raised doubts as to whether the wedding ought to be postponed.

However, my father would have none of that. With his arm in a sling we walked up the aisle of Wilton church together on the appointed day. I do not know what his heart was doing just then, but I know my own was bouncing around in the most extraordinary manner. It was the same church in which my parents had been married twenty-seven years before. My father and I were not often in church together, although he used to accompany me sometimes when I was a child. No one could exactly call him a religious man, but I know he had a simple faith in a power higher than mankind, one which made seeds grow and corn ripen. Once, when I was away doing my initial training in the A.T.S. he wrote to me, saying, "Do you mind if I finish in the same way as my father did in his first letter to me when I was in Canada? 'May the Great Architect of the Universe have you in his keeping.' "

My father was in great pain during my wedding ceremony due to his arm, which had already been broken twice in his life and was always stiff, and unfortunately this latest injury was to give him trouble for some long time to come. But he was always a man to discount disabilities. "In life," he would say, "the great thing is to keep on keeping on. The worst mistake is to give up. Always remember that tomorrow is so much more important than yesterday."

After my marriage my husband came out of the army and went back to his pre-war job in the City, but in 1948 he asked my father what his prospects might be if he went in for farming. Having been a prisoner-of-war for three and a half years, he felt he did not want to spend the rest of his life cooped up in an office. I suppose my father's feelings about the matter must have been very mixed. He knew that my husband did not know wheat from barley or an Ayrshire cow from a Friesian. He knew that he did not possess very much capital to invest, and the risk was obviously very great. On the other hand, he was always willing to help anyone 'have a go'. He reckoned that young people were like unbroken colts. One could never do anything with the ones who dug their heels in and refused to 'go'; but one could do anything with the ones who would.

The matter was discussed at great length by all the family, and finally my father promised to look around and see if there were any suitable farms for sale in the neighbourhood. For obvious reasons, it would have to be one within striking distance of his own farm, as he had promised to look after us for a year and must therefore be near at hand. Besides this, he would be able to lend us implements, because, of sheer necessity, we would only be able to buy the very minimum with which to start.

Two farms came on the market during the spring of 1948, and my father went into the pros and cons of each with great deliberation. My husband knew virtually nothing, and when I think of the young men today who, even with sufficient capital, need a degree before they can go into such a competitive and complicated business, it seems incredible that we ever entertained the idea. But then, I suppose, my husband had a very unusual and extremely able sponsor and tutor, and he, himself, proved to be an apt pupil. Afterwards my father always used to refer to the venture as his "magnum opus".

Eventually the overall advantages of one of the two farms tipped the scales, and my father negotiated the deal. My husband put up a third of the capital; the rest we borrowed from the Agricultural Mortgage Society. After my father had bought the Manor Farm, Steeple Langford, on our behalf, I understand he went home feeling sick. He never liked dealing in large sums of money, and now he had pledged somebody else's. The enormity of the undertaking must have hit him so that even his enthusiastic optimism was open to doubts. However, with characteristic foresight,

Ditchampton Farm.

My father planning the first improvements to Mill Farm.

In his new study at Mill Farm.

he still encouraged us to go on a holiday which had been planned some time previously, because, he said, "You might as well go now. You may never get another one for a very long time."

We came down to Wiltshire in September 1948 and lived with my parents until we were able to move into our new home. They gave us every help and encouragement. One night, when some new heifers arrived for us at the station, I remember sitting in the car with my father, whilst, in semi-darkness, my husband chivvied the last reluctant animal through thick mud at the entrance to one of our fields. It seemed to me to be a far cry from Threadneedle Street, and my father must have been thinking much on the same lines. "Bless my soul," he remarked, "I never thought to see that young man doing anything like this. Isn't it wonderful?"

Our first year's farming, though fraught with the usual ups and downs, was an unprecedented success. I have never been a good farmer's daughter nor a good farmer's wife, in that the technicalities of the whole thing escape me; in fact, I was very dubious about this whole new undertaking. I suppose I was brought up in an era when one vaguely absorbed what was happening on the farming side of life, but otherwise women kept strictly to the domestic front. But I knew now, of course, that my father was always about on our farm, keeping a watching brief, suggesting to my husband (but not telling him) what should or should not be done, and what is more 'when'. Moreover, he did not forget what was happening on the home front as well.

The day we actually moved into our house, Charlie Noble was instructed to drive a tractor and trailer to Steeple Langford with our few belongings, which my parents had been storing and helping us to accumulate, but there was so little that the whole load was brought in through the french windows and deposited in one room. I must say I began to feel very depressed. What had been sufficient in a two-roomed London flat did not go very far in our new home, in spite of the fact that the latter was quite small also. We spread everything around as far as we were able, but it seemed as though I was continually having to go off and buy certain items, such as a kitchen chair or a small milk churn, for our daily requirements.

After a while, my father decided I was lonely. He kept my husband working so hard that he felt I must be needing some company. One day he appeared with a beautiful little pedigree cocker spaniel puppy. Marcus was delightful, except that he gave me a great deal more work. But as work, in my father's opinion, was always a good antidote for most of nature's ills, Marcus certainly fulfilled his duty. He was not house-trained, and he had a great desire for the outdoors. Unfortunately, however, we came in for a particularly wet spell just after his arrival. As we lived near a main road and my husband was always driving in and out of the front gate in a tearing hurry, it meant either keeping the gate shut, thereby holding up farming operations, or taking Marcus out on a lead in the pouring rain to satisfy nature's needs and his own insatiable desire to sniff the good earth. It seemed as if I spent my entire days catering for Marcus' whims and washing my kitchen floor, as however hard I tried to clean his feet after every sortie I was never wholly successful.

One Sunday evening, when it had been raining all day, a wet patch appeared on our bedroom ceiling. My husband disappeared through the small trap-door into the attic and discovered that it was not the roof but the cistern which was leaking. I felt even more dismal at this latest discovery, and when my mother telephoned a little later I ended up by saying, "And to crown everything, now the cistern's bust."

About half an hour later, the headlights of a car shone through our gateway, and soon my father was standing on the doorstep. "I just came to tell you," he said, as he clambered up the stairs to view the damage, "that, in my experience, a little bit of soap applied to the place in the cistern where the drips are coming from will tide you over until you can get the plumber in the morning." He then regretted that his increasing girth prevented him from getting up into the roof himself and came downstairs to talk about everything else under the sun. He may easily have been tired that evening, as Sunday was the day he always reckoned on writing his *Farmers Weekly* article, but he always had a genius for knowing when a personal visit would be most appreciated. He reckoned there were times in life when a letter was necessary; there were times when a telephone call would do the trick; but there were also times when neither of these forms of communication were any good at all. This was one of them.

From the farming point of view, the weather was exceptionally kind to us during that first year. The heavens opened to let down the necessary rain when needed, and the sun shone appropriately at other times. My husband made better hay during the summer of 1949 than in any other year since. But there was one development which took place just then, unconnected with farming, but which nevertheless had enormous repercussions on all our lives. On New Year's Day I was fairly certain I was pregnant.

We waited until there was no doubt at all and then informed the family. The news rather shook my father. This was certainly something not even he had legislated for when contemplating the eventualities of our new mode of life. Secretly, I think he was tremendously pleased, but he also thought that it was something which might well have been postponed until we were a little more firmly established.

It was touch and go whether his coming grandchild would be born during harvest, when I think he was afraid that farming operations might become complicated. However, owing to single-minded efforts on all sides, carried on under a most obliging sun, all our corn was safely gathered in before the end of August, just a few days before his grand-daughter, most accommodatingly, made her début on the scene.

My father came to visit me in the hospital where she was born, and where, in the same room, seventeen years later, he was to fight his last battle. He was 57 when he became a grandfather for the first and only time, and he had had quite a year one way and another. I suppose I thought of him as quite old, as a younger generation always does look upon an older one, but his zest for life was undiminished. He was undoubtedly delighted with the way things had all worked out.

True to the promise which he had made the previous summer, he now announced that he was going to cease to give advice about farming, unless it was specifically asked for, because he reckoned a man only learnt by making his own mistakes. He was just going to sit back and see what happened. It must have been a difficult role for him to take on. He had become so interested in our farm. He had always wanted to own a little bit of England, and he used to joke with us that we had become landowners whilst he remained a tenant farmer. But, true to his word, after the end of our first farming year, he never came to see the farm unless invited; he never told my husband what he should or should not be doing; yet if we ever asked about anything, we were the fortunate consumers on the receiving end of his vast store of knowledge and common sense.

I know of no better way to describe the rather special achievements of that year than to quote from a letter I found in one of my father's files shortly after his death. It was written by my husband and dated 25th August, 1949. It is a long letter, and I shall not repeat it all, but certain extracts speak for themselves:

> . . . and here I must thank you for your wonderful tolerance and patience. . . . Many a time you have painstakingly explained farming procedure to me to pass on to my men, when it would have been far easier for you to drive down to Steeple Langford and tell the men what to do yourself . . . for the sheer drudgery of filling up another's countless forms . . . for your friendly counsel in assisting me towards appreciation and correct valuation of country life and sport. . . . You have enabled me to fit myself into a job that seems worthwhile. . . . I don't think at the time I fully realized how much I was asking of you, and I rather doubt that you quite realized to how much time and worry you were committing yourself . . . even planning your own farming to fit in with mine so that this could be done to my greatest advantage.

CHAPTER SEVEN

"I was a farmer long before I was a scribbler."
A.G.S. *Country Calendar*
"I have no diplomas or certificates in the bottom of my trunk."
A.G.S. *Hedgetrimmings*

I feel, perhaps, that I have not written enough about my father's literary and broadcasting work. Maybe I have dwelt too much on his role as a father and a farmer, but not enough on the other side of his life. All my father's files connected with this were kept in his filing cabinet under the simple heading of WORK. He much preferred it to the word LITERARY.

"By the time you've written a book," he once said to me, "and read it and corrected it and read it again, and then done the same things with the proofs, you're sick and tired of the darned thing. I admit I was lucky in the beginning, luckier than I deserve, but the great thing is to recognize luck when it comes along and play it for all you are worth. In my case, 'playing it' meant WORK."

In my attic now I have the tangible record of that day-to-day work, going back as far as 1929. I have also, in my safe, the two grocer's order books in which my father wrote *Farmer's Glory* with the stub of a pencil. These books must have been spare left-overs from the days when my father, amongst all his other activities, took on a grocery business known as the 'Four Corners' in Wilton. Little did he dream that one day these books, with their headed and perforated pages advertising home-cured bacon, would be on exhibit at the *Sunday Times* Book Exhibition to show how the original draft of *Farmer's Glory* was written.

The manuscripts of all my father's other books are type-written and stacked in an old wooden box. He wrote thirty-five books in all in the space of thirty-four years, not bad going for a man who hardly put pen to paper before he was 40. The piles of reviews of these books seem countless. A few are bad, most are good, and some are superlative, especially those of *Farmer's Glory* and all his early novels, besides the books of essays and broadcast talks such as *Country Days, Country Calendar* and *Thinking Aloud.* My mother treasures a photostat copy of the frontispiece of *Country Calendar,* on which is written in the late Queen Mary's handwriting:

The King was reading this book
at the time of his last illness.
Mary R.
For the Windsor library.

In the bottom of one box of papers I have discovered an old green scrap-book. The first article my father ever wrote has been pasted in at the beginning, the one which the *Daily Mail* published in 1929 and which sowed the seeds of his literary career. There is a faded photograph of him halfway down one column. He looks incredibly young and appears to be wearing a wing-collar, something I never remember seeing him in, but there are the straight penetrating eyes which I knew so well and which always seemed to look right through one and beyond.

The article starts off in true characteristic fashion : "Most of those who are writing about the present agricultural depression are suggesting that somebody or other should do something for agriculture, never that agriculture should do something for itself." He then goes on to say, "A generation of farmers must arise who can get a living as farmers in spite of any Government rather than with the aid of any Government's intervention." At the end of the article my father has written in ink in large letters "£3. 3. 0." How pleased he must have been.

The next article to be pasted in was one written in the *Sunday Chronicle* in March 1930. This was shorter and was more of a skit on the government, and the figures "£2. 2. 0." are written at the bottom. Then there is a varied crop of articles, published here, there and everywhere, but mostly in the local paper, some fetching as little as seven and sixpence. But my father evidently lived up to his maxim of "keeping on keeping on", because towards the end of the book the same sort of article appears to be fetching seventeen shillings and sixpence.

I also have bundle upon bundle of large envelopes containing the printed articles cut from the *Farmers Weekly*, which my father started as far back as 1935. I see a photograph of my father and myself on horseback tucked away in a corner of one page on 7th June of that year. My beloved Toby has his ears cocked forward, and I am glad to see how his coat shines out, in spite of the faded yellowing paper.

A year later, my father's *Random Philosophy* articles take up a whole page, whilst on 18th December 1936 there appears to be a double page devoted to Christmas greetings from my father, on behalf of the paper, to all British farmers. These end up with the words:

> And to all the farming folk of Britain, and especially to those whom we may have omitted to mention, we here send our sincere greetings. We know that on Christmas morning farm work must still be done; that the shepherd must tend his flock; that in the dark of the early morning the dairyman's lantern must flicker across the yards and also over the rolling downs; that the pigs and hens and horses in every county must be fed; and that Christmas will bring little leisure to the majority of farming folk. We know also that these things will be done properly, and that the farming community of Britain throughout the Christmas holiday and afterwards, will continue to shoulder its responsibility as the trustees of the nation's one permanent asset, the land. To all we send our Christmas greetings, and the assurance that we will do our best to serve them as faithfully as they serve the nation.

There is also a multitude of other press cuttings from national newspapers and magazines; there is a report of one of Foyle's literary luncheons in 1933 when H. G. Wells spoke on 'Intolerance', and my father had to reply to Professor Laski's toast of 'Literature and Intelligence'; and there are letters, hundreds and hundreds of them. I started to go through them all soon after my father's death and it seemed a monumental task. The ordinary ones I must throw away sometime, but there are a few personal ones which I should like to keep.

My attic also holds records of the most tremendous amount of detailed research which my father did before writing some of his novels. He was always a stickler for getting his facts correct. If he was writing about a horse being shipped to the Continent for one reason or another, as he did in *A Crook in the Furrow,* then he took great pains to find out exactly how this was done. I was amazed to discover all the correspondence that went on between him and officials in the Canadian Government before he started on his novel *Cooper's Crossing*. At the end of any research work of this kind, there is always a copy of a courteous letter from my father thanking whomsoever had given him the necessary information.

The first record I have of my father doing any broadcasting is from the *Manchester Guardian* in 1933. It is written by someone signed K.H., who says, "Mr. Street's descriptions create in a few seemingly casual sentences a detailed panorama of the country scene described. He has, too, an insight, an understanding of man and beast which informs his talks with a rich humanity. . . . Everything he touches, lives. He is always full of human interest, and is a fascinating story-teller." It is strange to think that only a few years before this he was listening to popular programmes on that home-made wireless set he had made with his nephew, little dreaming that he would soon be in demand himself as a broadcaster.

My father also did quite a bit of television work from time to time, and just before the war he once took me with him to the studios at Alexandra Palace. I think possibly, however, I was more impressed by the fact that my father stoically continued to go on talking when the cameras blew up in front of him, than with the actual programme. The producer and technicians were delighted with him, as it meant the sound, at least, continued.

I think, undoubtedly, my father's greatest fame in broadcasting came when he was asked in 1949 to take part in a new radio programme which had just started called "Any Questions". He was to be a member of a panel of four experts in various walks of life, who, every Friday evening, visited certain towns in the south and west of England and, as the name implies, virtually answered any questions. Freddie Grisewood was the travelling questionmaster, and the programme proved to be a great success and is still taking place to this day.

My father enjoyed this particular form of broadcasting and unquestionably had a flair for it. He became one of the team's 'regulars', and, unless there was some specific question on agriculture, Freddie Grisewood usually left him to the last, when he would place the ball firmly in my father's court saying something like, "Now, A.G., what have you got to say?" What my father had to say was usually full of common sense and extremely funny, and we who were listening at home usually reckoned on him bringing the house down at least once during a session.

A little while ago, Michael Bowen, the producer of "Any Questions", devised a programme called "Portrait of a Countryman", which was a kind of tribute to the memory of my father. When it was completed, he kindly asked me to go down to the B.B.C. at Bristol and listen to a pre-recording before it went out over the air. I went with some misgivings. I thought it would be extremely harrowing to hear my father's voice again, and I hardly knew how I should feel. But I was very pleasantly surprised. I found I was still able to laugh with him over some of his wittier remarks made on a previous "Any Questions" programme, and I felt very grateful to Michael Bowen for doing such a good job, one which I understand was more of a labour of love, and one which I felt sure my father would have approved of also.

The programme was so popular that it was repeated again shortly afterwards, and I received many letters about it from complete strangers. "Everything your father wrote or said," wrote one lady, "was such an antidote to drift, dullness, and drivel, which threatens to overwhelm us at times—and in enjoying life, he enriched it for everybody."

My father did enjoy life. There was no doubt about that. He worked hard, but, except during the farming depression, when he had his back to the wall, he also played hard. He lived life to the full, and, even when he appeared to be doing nothing very much, his active brain was usually working overtime thinking out the plot for his next book. Then he would get down to business. He always liked to think of a title fairly early on in proceedings. That, he said, gave him a peg to hang his thoughts on. Then he would sit down, put a blank sheet of paper in his typewriter and start banging away. He always said it was surprising the ideas which came once one sat down and, "tucked the desk into one's tummy".

My crowded attic brings back the memory of years I thought I had forgotten, but the thing which hits me so forcibly, as I delve into the various packages, is the sheer volume of work which my father accomplished. There is a sadness in the dusty manuscripts and tattered files, but there is also a comforting strength; and I know, as I undo the string tying up the typewritten sheets of this or that book, that on countless book-shelves in libraries and homes all over the world, there are the successful printed and published results of hours and hours of sheer hard work, put in by a man whose simple sincerity came through with every word he wrote.

When he died, my father left instructions that there was to be no memorial service of any kind for him. My mother received thousands of letters after his death, but one stands out above all the rest. It is from a neighbouring farmer and ends, ". . . he has created his own memorial in his lifetime."

CHAPTER EIGHT

> "Every man has his secret desire, I suppose, and mine is some day to own a farm."
>
> A.G.S. *Country Calendar*

In 1951 my father left Ditchampton Farm. He had farmed it since 1918, he had written about it, and he had loved it. He was now nearly 60, and it was no small decision to have to make. But the growth of new housing estates over its one-time peaceful fields was more than he could bear. He was once again, as he was wont to say, "force put".

For both my parents it was an enormous wrench. They had transformed the house from a somewhat utilitarian Victorian residence into something which had charm and character, and for my mother, especially, leaving the home and garden which she had done so much to create, was a heart-breaking affair.

My father toyed with the idea of buying a farm to the south of Salisbury, but when the Earl of Pembroke gave him the offer of another farm which had just become vacant on the estate, he decided to accept it. This was on the opposite side of the Wylye Valley to Ditchampton, and my father seemed quite certain that Mill Farm, as it was called, would be a very good one by the time he had got things under control, especially as it was not likely to be subjected to any building programmes. But the farm-house itself was even more of a difficult proposition than Ditchampton had been before it was altered. However, with boyish enthusiasm, my father sat down straight away on a ladder in his home-to-be and proceeded to make plans to turn the whole place inside out.

For a start, he decided that the front staircase was to be abolished completely. We were even afraid at one point that he intended to install a lift and nothing else. Next, a larger drawing-room needed to be planned; then the existing dining-room and study were changed about, so that no one could spy him out on arrival at the front door; the kitchen was then replanned and made up-to-date to assist the long-suffering Vivi; a second bathroom was to be created next to my mother and father's bedroom; and, lastly, my mother was promised that the whole of the farm staff would come into the garden whenever she gave the word, in order to attack the wilderness which was driving her into a fit of depression. My father knew that farming at Ditchampton had become practically impossible, he knew he had to move, but he also knew just what all this meant to his 'womenfolk' and he was doing his best to make things easier for them.

My father was very chivalrous towards women and had very definite ideas about what they should or should not do, especially the ones in his own household. Although my mother and Vivi spoilt him in many ways, he, in return, also spoilt them. There were two things of which he disapproved strongly. He did not like either of them being left alone in a house at night; he did not approve of them catching buses. I can hear him now giving orders to Brian Wiltshire, the man who worked for him devotedly for twenty years, ever since the age of 16. "Brian," he would say, "I want you to drive Miss Boon (this was Vivi) to Salisbury shopping. She will have a lot of parcels. You must wait on her."

I was always surprised that, considering what a busy man he was himself, how extraordinarily patient he could be when waiting in a car for one or another of us. "I study form," he once said to me when we were waiting together and a rather anaemic-looking lady passed by. "Now I wouldn't give fourpence for that one. Not a good 'doer', as they say. I'm a stockman. I should know." He was always interested in everything and everybody.

As the years rolled by, Brian's position in the household became unique. During the time he spent with my father he was at one period or another farm-worker, gardener, handy man, chauffeur, electrician, interior decorator, gillie, loader, foreman and, in those last tragic months when my father was so ill and so heavy to lift, male nurse. He slept in the same room as my father just before he was taken to hospital. In the mornings I might say to Brian, "What sort of a night did you have?"

"Oh, not too bad on the whole," he would reply in his slow Wiltshire dialect. "We talked a bit about old times up 'til twelve o'clock or so. On about shooting, he was. And after that he settled down nicely."

"Did you get any sleep yourself?" I would ask, knowing in his conscientious way he had probably kept one ear open in case my father should try and get out of bed unaided.

"Oh yes, I got plenty enough. You don't need to worry about I. If you want me at any time today, just give a shout.

Mill Farm. My mother and father in the drawing-room.

Outside the inn. My father used to say that most of the pleasure-able things in life are seldom planned.

Shooting with the ever-faithful Brian in attendance.

I shan't be far away," and off he would go to see to this or that, because he was foreman now as well as everything else. But he arranged the work on the farm so that no matter what time of day, he himself was available to do anything we wanted.

Once, during my father's last illness, in one of his more lucid moments, he talked to me about Brian. "I suppose it's all very wrong," he said, "especially in this day and age, to have this personal servant relationship. I suppose it's very bad for me to have had a 'Brian' always on hand."

I looked at him lying in the bed. He had got thinner now, and his face was drawn. I shook my head. He knew that I was capable of having somewhat Leftish views at times, but I also knew that there was precious little wrong with a relationship such as his and Brian's, a relationship so loyal that when we tried to persuade Brian to take his annual holiday when my father was in hospital, in order to be fit to manage the forthcoming harvest, he said, "It's just that I wouldn't like to be away if Mr. Street should need me or," and here his voice faltered, "if anything should happen, I want to be there when he goes on his last journey."

That sort of relationship is more or less out of date now. In fact my father often used to say in latter years that he had outlived his time and the world had passed him by. When Michael Bowen, the producer of "Any Questions", came to see me to ask a few details before working on the programme about my father's life, we discussed who would be best to go on the air and talk about him. Brian, of course, came first to my mind, and I gave Michael the names of about half a dozen others, but sadly I realized that many of my father's contemporaries had died also. I remembered the fiery old farmer who used to come and 'put the world straight' with him in my youth; I thought of Reginald Arkell and many of the other Savages who had been such good friends of his; I thought of the old dairyman we used to have at Ditchampton Farm on whom the book *The Gentleman of the Party* was based.

"I'm sorry, Michael," I said at last, "but so many of them are gone too." He nodded and got up to go.

"I know," he said, and then, as he went out of the door, he stopped and added, "Your father was unique you know. They don't make them like him any more. There are no A.G.s coming along."

It did seem as if my father had a personal magnetism which injected his own special brand of common sense, loyalty and good humour into most people with whom he came in contact. Certainly the latter attribute seemed to overtake the builders when they were doing the alterations to Mill Farm. They became aware that Brian amongst all his other activities, was a would-be mushroom cultivator. Thinking that the cellars of this new house might be excellent for the purpose, he sowed spawn in several boxes, and during the big move, every time he arrived at Mill Farm on some errand or other, he went off down to the cellar, anxiously looking for results. One day, on my father's instructions, the workmen removed several of the inside doors of the house. With great cunning, they took off the shiny white door-knobs and placed them strategically on Brian's mushroom beds. When next he went to investigate, it looked as if the results far exceeded his wildest expectations, until, on closer inspection, he realized what had happened and joined in the general hilarity.

On completion of the alterations, the workmen left Mill Farm much improved, although I, personally, never found the place, in spite of all my parents' efforts, as attractive as Ditchampton had been. Maybe this was because it held no childhood memories for me. There were no bushy laurels in which I used to play; there were no loose-boxes close at hand, from which horses heads used to pop out whenever my father or I lifted the latch of the farmyard gate. Even the cellars in which Brian had tried to succeed as a mushroom grower were not like the large water-logged rooms, where I used to splash about in gum-boots catching newts underneath the kitchen of Ditchampton Farm. My daughter may well possess cherished secrets of Mill Farm of which I know nothing, for she certainly spent much time there when she was young; but for me, as I pass by and look up at the windows and wonder about the people now living there, there is only a sadness and a wish to forget those last distressing weeks when we watched my father become so ill.

There was no doubt, however, that in 1951 the move had been a sound one. With his customary efficiency, my father soon had the farm in good working order, but he did it in such a way as to give himself the least possible worry. He kept no livestock except a few steers, and he had long ago given up the idea of running a dairy herd. After being a slave to cows for so many years during the hard times, it gave him great satisfaction to hear the clinking of milk bottles as they were brought to his own doorstep every day. Although his enthusiasm and interest in farming never waned right until the end, I think in his heart of hearts he was well aware he was getting older, and the thought of old age depressed him.

Unfortunately, for private domestic reasons, Charlie Noble, the foreman, did not make the move to Mill Farm with him, so my father, at the age of 60, started off not only with a new farm but also with a new foreman. However, soon the organization was such that everything was running according to plan, or, to use another of his own well-known Wiltshire expressions, "suently". He seemed to be able to manage the farm with one finger; start work on another book, write his regular *Farmers Weekly* articles and a great deal of other journalism as well; take part regularly in "Any Questions", assist MacDonald Hastings in the publication of *Country Fair*, the magazine they started together; and, with the ever-faithful Brian in attendance, also find time for shooting and fishing, as well as driving himself into a club in Salisbury on certain evenings to play bridge. Later on, when the years caught up with him, Brian performed this task also, driving my father to the club about seven in the evenings and returning to fetch him about ten-thirty.

Some years after he moved to Mill Farm, my father acquired a further addition to his commitments. He actually purchased about forty acres of land on the outskirts of Salisbury. This seemed perhaps, a surprising thing for him to do after settling at Mill Farm, until one remembered how he had always wanted to own "a little bit of England". He knew that at his time of life he would never buy another farm; he knew that he would be unlikely ever to make another move, but these two fields, together with a small house and a few buildings, near Salisbury, seemed to him to be the nearest he would now get to his cherished dream. He farmed it from Mill Farm, sending men and equipment all along the main roads practically into Salisbury whenever they were required.

Although my mother left Mill Farm soon after my father died, she still possesses 'Cowslip', as this little acreage is called. A contractor does the farming, but my mother is, in name at least, the 'farmer'. We go there sometimes to see how things are getting on. The houses of Salisbury sprawl round us in three directions. To the north the green rings of Old Sarum stand guard on the other side of the river Avon; to the east the spire of Salisbury Cathedral points upwards in its never-changing majesty, and my father's "little bit of England", according to the seasons, turns brown, green, and golden, as the corn is sown, grown, and harvested in a way of which I hope he would approve.

CHAPTER NINE

> "The only advice I can give you is to trust your hunches. Big decisions should never be settled solely on logical grounds. The deciding factor should be if a bell rings somewhere in your inner consciousness telling you that in spite of logic, this or that procedure is the right one."
>
> Letter from A.G.S. to P.S. 1946

In the summer of 1954 the trains still stopped at Wylye station, the nearest one to where we lived. The axe which Dr. Beeching was to wield had yet to fall on the little ticket office and waiting-room that are now no more than a few weeds and pieces of rubble. My father suddenly became aware that his grand-daughter had never experienced this kind of travel.

"God bless my soul," he said to me, "you've neglected the child's education. This must be put right at once." The next evening after tea, two figures, one very large and one very small, could be seen purchasing tickets there for the sole but infinitely exciting purpose of travelling six miles to Wilton, where my husband had been detailed to collect them.

It would be hard to say which of them enjoyed the

journey most. In those days, I think my daughter regarded her grandfather as an enormously safe and benevolent kind of bear, who was the instigator of frequent adventures of a most unusual kind. Needless to say, she has gone on countless other journeys since then, a great many by air, a mode of transport which her grandfather only undertook once when he went on a fishing trip to Ireland, but I doubt whether any of them meant quite as much to her as this impromptu expedition through the Wylye Valley when she was nearly 5 years old.

A year later she spent a whole summer at Mill Farm, and my father became, amongst all his other activities, an unusually conscientious nursemaid. My husband had been ill, so ill in fact that more than one doctor advised him not only to go on a long holiday but also to consider giving up farming altogether. As it turned out, the latter advice was quite unnecessary and based on far too gloomy a prognosis.

We had been farming for seven years now and getting a little more established with each one that passed. However, to go away completely for any length of time posed tremendous problems. But where one is 'force put', there are always unexpected ways of managing things which under ordinary circumstances look like being impossible. At the beginning of my husband's illness my father took over the running of our farm, and one of his letters to my husband in February of that year ends in typical fashion: "For your information, last Saturday, cold as hell, you sent off 250 gallons of milk. Where it comes from I'm damned if I know!"

But it was obvious that if we were to go away on a "slow boat to South Africa", which was actually what one rather imaginative doctor recommended, my father, who was now nearing 63, could not be expected to take on our farm again for a somewhat indefinite period, in spite of the fact that another of his letters at that time ended, "If there is anything else you want me to do, just ring up or write. For the rest, you stay put and sleep all you can. There's nothing like it."

We had employed no secretary in those days, my husband doing all the office work, and now, to add to our other predicaments our foreman had suddenly been offered the chance to fulfil a lifelong ambition, a smallholding of his own, which meant looking around for another man to take his place. In the end we managed to arrange for a friendly neighbour, who owned the farm next to us, to take on the whole running of our farm, whilst my father held a watching brief in the background. But he was certainly nowhere in the background as far as his grand-daughter was concerned. She went to stay with her grandparents for the whole summer. There is a place on the river Wylye, which in 1955 became christened 'Wishford Beach', and it was here, whenever he had a free hour and the weather was fine, he took his grand-daughter and watched whilst she paddled or fished for minnows. On arriving home again, he would meticulously inform my mother that he, personally, had seen to it that her feet had been well and truly dried.

A little while ago my daughter started talking to me about that summer. She said she would never forget the comfort it was to have, in our absence, this big burly man taking her about with him whenever he could. He seemed so strong, so decisive, such an authority on everything, that she felt if anything had happened to him her world would collapse.

But it was not only his grand-daughter who thought like

that; so many others felt his strength. One could always count on him; so that when, suddenly, he was no longer with us, when his study was empty and there was no one sitting at the large desk by the window, no eyes raised in welcome, no voice saying, "Come in, my dear, how nice to see you," no one to ask for an opinion which one knew would be well-considered, however trivial and unimportant it was, it seemed as if the whole world was a lonelier and more bewildering place.

I never realized until he had gone how much I owed my father or how much I loved him. I had argued with him violently in my youth; I had disagreed with many things he stood for, whilst, at the same time, I had taken for granted so much of his help and counsel. But when that wise counsel and advice was no longer forthcoming, it came as the greatest shock to find that others were turning to me for a final decision on something which he, automatically, would have pronounced judgment on in the past.

Seemingly simple things, like putting the announcements of his death in the newspapers, proved not so simple after all. There was so little time, and they had to be worded correctly. Within ten minutes of his death, Pressmen were asking questions, and, as his obituaries would be appearing the following day, we wanted the announcements in the paper also. It seemed impossible that he was not there to ask if our wording was, at the least, satisfactory. He always had such an infallible way of knowing what was right and expected. I longed to ring him up and say, "Is it O.K. by you if, in the same announcement, we put in about your not wanting any memorial service?"

But he just was not there to ask, and I had, perhaps for the first time in my life, to sit down and really think. I have never been very logical, but it seemed to me that, as he had made it so easy for us with his straightforward funeral instructions which he had written some years prior to his death, so we must make it now as easy for his friends. Therefore the words went in: "There will be no memorial service at his special request." That way they would all know where they were at once, which is what he would have wanted.

But alongside his desire to have everything cut and dried, there was a very strong sentimental streak in his make-up. Sometimes people who had not understood why he had done some quixotic action, might say, "But why, A.G., why?" And my father would reply, "Oh, just because." There always seemed a wealth of explanation in those three words.

It was 'just because' that, when any of us had gone to London for a day's shopping and he was going to meet us at the station in the evening, we could always count on seeing his large square figure standing on the platform instead of simply sitting in the car until we came out into the station yard.

It was 'just because' that I received a mammoth bottle of Chanel No. 5 after accompanying my mother and father to London on the very last journey he ever made there. My mother had to see a doctor, and my father was determined to go with her, but he was obviously not looking forward to the trip. He was none too steady on his feet now, and getting in and out of trains and taxis was a tremendously difficult task for him. I suggested going with them, and he seemed to be relieved. I never realized just how hard it was for him until we arrived at Waterloo. It took him a very long time to get down on to the platform, carefully placing his poor feet sideways on the narrow step of the train door.

We had a successful visit to the doctor, but in the taxi going down Regent Street, on the way back to Waterloo, he remarked rather wistfully that the Savage Club had moved to new premises in Covent Garden which he had never seen. I suggested we made a detour and he paid his brother Savages a visit, but he shook his head. "It's a long time since I did that. I'm too old, my dear. There may be no one I know, and besides, it would mean getting out and into another taxi." He glanced to the left down one or two streets as we neared Piccadilly, and I felt like crying.

How many years ago was it that he took his grand-daughter on her first rail trip? Only eleven, but time was certainly not waiting for him now. He had already given us one bad scare the previous year. Whilst he was out shooting he was taken ill, and Brian had to bring him home. A specialist thought there had been a kind of ballooning of an artery in his head, but that he was lucky because it had subsided. Although many people never expected to see him out shooting again, there he was during the season of 1965, going off with Brian, eager as ever, with the most curious and original seat, which the latter had constructed for him on the bonnet of his Land Rover and which enabled him to sit down and fire away.

We had moved house by then and added a little more land to our existing farm. Whenever there was a shoot, my father and Brian were the 'regulars' in the party. But if there was sometimes a dearth of birds, there was certainly no lack of conversation during mealtimes when he was about. There was, I think, a great deal of pleasurable disagreement, for whatever my father said was usually controversial. He would arrive, like some large green space-man, more often than not clad from head to foot in waterproof clothing, and fire, not only with his gun but also with his tongue, shooting some highly original thought across the dining-table at lunch, and soon reports were thundering back so that it was almost impossible to hear oneself speak.

At the end of the day he would thank us courteously, stump out of the door, heave himself up into the Land Rover, assisted by Brian, and they would drive away. They were a unique pair, those two. How could one know that cold January day of 1966 it was the last time they would ever drive off from our house together after a day's shooting. One knew, perhaps, that it would not go on much longer, but one stifled the thought. In any case, they seemed so indestructible as they disappeared into the night, for all the world like Tweedle-dum and Tweedle-dee.

CHAPTER TEN

> "In looking back on my life, the bulk of the worth-while things in it are connected with friendship."
>
> A.G.S. *Farmer's Glory*
>
> "Any attempt to judge a man either by his politics, his social class, or his calling has always been to me like a red rag to a bull."
>
> A.G.S. *Wessex Wins*

I suppose most of us who knew my father well had been uneasy about his health for some considerable time, but, because he was a man who had learnt so successfully to overcome physical handicaps since his youth, we accepted the fact that, even after as severe a set-back as the one when Brian brought him home in the middle of a day's shooting, he was often back in circulation again in a surprisingly short time. "Surfacing" was the word he was in the habit of using for his reappearance in society. One day he would be in bed and my mother would insist on sending for the doctor, and the next he would be out and about again, with his 'womenfolk' on the doorstep, waving scarves and imploring him to come back indoors and remain in his study, at least. Rather like Toddie in *Helen's Babies*, he had given everyone a bad fright, and now he was in the dog-house. But he was never there for very long.

Somehow, it was difficult to stay angry with my father for any length of time. He could argue with you; he could infuriate you; he would appear to be quite impossible about something or other, and then he would completely disarm you by saying he was sorry. He really meant it too. If he was in the wrong, he admitted it and was absolutely sincere in his apologies. But he was not a man who was wrong very often; he was, perhaps, more often infuriatingly right, but one had to hand it to him. He always stood his ground on a question of a principle which he was convinced was the right one. "Ideas," he used to say, "are things which you hold. Convictions are things which hold you."

I think one of the nicest things about my father was that he 'cared' so much about everything. There was never any lack of reaction to something one might say. He always had all sorts of original theories, whether they were to do with growing sugar-beet or driving steam-rollers. One thing he could never be was dull. I remember him once giving a pound to a man who was working a steam-roller on one of our farm roads and saying, "I've wanted to get the feel of one of these things all my life." He then solemnly exchanged places with the driver and rolled up to the house in triumph in time for lunch.

My father had an absolutely simple straightforward code of what was right and what was wrong, what was 'done' and what was 'not done', according to a true countryman's standards. He had no time for people who just did the 'done' thing in the fashionable sense of the word, like putting the tea in the cup before the milk. Whenever he came to our house and I omitted to put his milk in first, he passed it on to someone else and asked for another cup. He maintained it tasted better his way, and the drink was more homogeneous. His 'done' or 'not done' things were much more basic, like keeping faith with his fellow men and not letting anyone down.

My father never 'kidded' anybody, least of all, himself. Sometimes, I might go to see him and produce what I thought was a valid reason for something I intended doing or not doing. After he had heard me out, he invariably knew whether the reasons I had put forward were the real ones or what I thought were my real ones. If he felt that I had not come out with what he called the 'whole works', he would sit back in his chair, smile, and say, "Well, my dear, who are you kidding? That's just a pipe dream."

He also had no time for people who were just being clever. He was the most adept of men at piercing any kind of façade. He would shake his head when confronted with pictures of modern art or sculpture, the ones perhaps with two eyes in the same side of the face, or a grotesque figure which seemed all out of proportion. "If I had that one on the farm," he would say, "I'd have to shoot it. What disease d'you think it's got?" Then he would rumble on a bit more and say, "You know, it's amazing about these Johnnies who create things like that. D'you think they really believe it's art themselves? Don't you think perhaps when they're meditating in their baths just looking at their big toes, the sort of time when a man's most likely to take stock of himself in more ways than one, they know, really, that they're just hoodwinking the public?"

As he grew older, most modern novels ceased to hold much attraction for him. He had always been a great reader, although I never knew how he found the time. He was always in and out of the libraries in Salisbury, but towards the end of his life, on arriving to see him, I might often be greeted with, "I say, read any good books lately?" And on leaving, he would enquire, "If you're on your way to Salisbury, would you have time to change my books? I can't read any of that lot."

If there was one author who gave my father the greatest enjoyment, I would say it was Kipling. He often quoted a line or two of his verses, especially the one from "The Land", where Kipling is writing of a village Hobden:

His dead are in the churchyard—thirty generations laid.
Their names were old in history when Domesday Book was made;
And the passion and the piety and prowess of his line
Have seeded, rooted, fruited in some land the Law calls mine.

In *A Choice of Kipling's Verse*, T. S. Eliot wrote about Kipling's "awareness" of places and atmosphere; that he had an "exceptional sensitiveness to environment," and that he never used "decoration for its own sake". The whole essay seemed to stress Kipling's gift for conveying a meaning in one reading or hearing. I think this is the quality which must have appealed to my father tremendously. I do not think it would be presumptuous to say that, besides appreciating Kipling's gifts to the full, my father perhaps shared with him a simplicity of purpose which got through to people in a way which no amount of seemingly clever description can ever do. "Never use a long word, when a shorter one will do," my father would say, "after all, it sounds so much nicer to 'begin' a book, rather than to 'commence' one."

He was beginning another book just before he became

A. G. Street the farmer. (*above*) Stooked oats. (*below*) Having ploughed the prairies in Manitoba as a young man, my father always regarded ploughing as the king of jobs.

Fishing at Testwood.

really ill. For some time now every book he had written was going to be his 'last', or so he thought at the time. Then the old leaven would start working again, and one day, sure enough, there he would be at his desk with Page 1, Chapter 1 rising up out of his typewriter. But *Unto the Third and Fourth Generation* was not going very well.

Apart from the occasions when he was more obviously unwell, there were other signs, almost imperceptible, especially to an outsider, that things were not right with him. It was the very nature of these somewhat covert symptoms which made them all the more sinister. Some were so slight that one wondered, perhaps, whether one had simply imagined that he had taken longer than usual to look up a word in a reference book. Had he just been joking when he said at the end of a television programme that he had not taken in a word of it? Anyone might back a car badly at times; or would they? Not my father, at least not until now.

He seemed to be spending a lot more time in bed, but perhaps that could be accounted for by the fact that he always said it was such a good place to be. He had always been a good sleeper and for many years he had taken to having an afternoon nap. "I'm going up to the horizontal," he would announce after lunch. It was nothing unheard of for him to go to bed at eight o'clock in the evening either, on occasions. There was now a television set in his bedroom, with a remote control switch so that he could turn it on and off from his bed.

It was 'just because' of all these signs that, whenever I was away, I felt it more necessary to leave word as to my exact whereabouts. In April 1966 I had to take my daughter to Italy, where she was going to stay with a family in

Verona. She had acquired a passion for languages other than her own. I think possibly this may have been a disappointment to my father, who believed, quite simply, that English was the best on earth, but he would never discourage a colt who wanted to 'go'. I noticed, however, that as he aged, he was enormously pleased to see any of us on our return to the fold again.

He was 74 on 7th April, and I put through a call from Italy to wish him many happy returns. The line was a bad one, and his voice seemed faint and almost feeble, I thought. It was nearly midday, but I gathered he was still in bed. "He seems so tired these days," my mother wrote in one of her letters.

As soon as I returned home, I went to see him. I happened to take a bus, and, in true characteristic fashion, he remarked, "Good Lord, fancy anyone catching a bus to see me." As soon as he came into the room I noticed there was a kind of grey look about him. Usually he was nice and pink.

I had brought my camera with me. I often think it was strange that I had been so keen to take a photograph of them all that day. I know it was not just because there was some film left on the spool. It somehow seemed very important to me to get a good picture. It was a fine evening; we all went outside, and they dutifully posed for me. I have the result on my desk beside me, and it is one of my better efforts. My father stands in the middle, looking straight into the camera, with my mother and Vivi on either side of him. But there is no doubt he looks far from well. Apart from his pallor, he is holding the arm which had always given him trouble as if he had it in a sling, because it had been more painful lately.

A week later they all came to Sunday lunch with us, and my father seemed unusually quiet. My husband drove him round our farm in the afternoon, something he always enjoyed, especially as he said it often gave him food for thought for his next *Farmers Weekly* article. He sometimes marvelled at a new road or some new installation of machinery which my husband had gone in for, shaking his head and saying his 'pupil' had outdistanced him.

The following Saturday my father was due to go fishing on the Test near Southampton. He woke up firmly convinced it was Friday, and my mother tried to dissuade him from going, but once he had got the day of the week straight in his mind, nothing would stop him and off he went with Brian. Just as they had done once before, when shooting, they arrived home unexpectedly. My father had suffered a semi-blackout, and Brian prevented him from walking straight into the river. When they were nearing Mill Farm he still hardly knew where he was.

The doctor was sent for. We were told his blood pressure was up and we must keep him as quiet as possible. But the next day, being Sunday, he was about again, trying to write his *Farmers Weekly* article. It was usually finished by twelve o'clock, but that day it was obvious that it never would be. His mind was working all right, working overtime perhaps, but he did not seem able to get his thoughts down on to paper. He had never been one to dictate, and it bothered him desperately. We begged him to give up trying, but he refused. There was something about the Government which he badly wanted to say.

I still have four sheets of typing paper covered with the last words which my father ever managed to write before he realized the article would never be ready on time. Much is crossed out, but there is one of his interesting and typical analogies which I have deciphered:

> Few of the farming powers that be are countrymen and therefore have not lived their lives as every countryman must do under the continuous and stringent scrutiny of their friends and neighbours. This sort of thing carries on even when a countryman is enjoying himself. For instance, consider Mr. A., Mr. B., and Mr. C., who are three guns at a shooting party. At the end of a certain drive, Mr. A. calls his keeper to one side and informs him that he has a bird down in a certain place. So does Mr. B. and also Mr. C. In Mr. A's case there is an immediate and careful search by the keepers and their dogs. In Mr. B's case much the same thing occurs; but Mr. C's information brings no comment, no search, but merely sardonic smiles. English countrymen don't waste their smiles, which mean they know that in Mr. C's case the information is unreliable. What I am driving at is that if any member of the powers that be in agriculture today was a member of a shooting party and told me he had a bird down, I shouldn't bother to send my dog and neither would any of the keepers. For repeatedly to disappoint a good gun dog soon blunts his keenness.

On Monday morning, when it was quite obvious that the article would never be finished in time to reach the *Farmers Weekly* offices in Fleet Street by the first post on Tuesday, something which had happened without fail for over thirty years, my father's secretary telephoned the Editor to that effect.

It was the beginning of the end.

CHAPTER ELEVEN

> "Of all the party the old dairyman had always been the most contented . . . alone amongst them he had always put the land first, and himself second."
>
> A.G.S. *The Gentleman of the Party*

I have hesitated before writing about the last month's of my father's life for two reasons. One is because he would have considered any report about his own health merely boring; he had, in fact, a healthy dislike of discussing his own ailments. The other reason is that it was such a very personal and poignant time for any of us who knew him so well. But I have tried, as honestly as I can, to paint a picture of my father as I saw him, and I saw a great deal of him during his last illness. Although there was great confusion in his mind, there was also great courage, and it seems as though this account of him would be incomplete without including in it how he came to die.

I know that I was closer to my father during those final weeks than at any other period of my life. There is much written today by sociologists about what they term the 'socialization' of children; that is to say, how much their characters are formed by environment or, in simpler terms, nurture, and how big a part nature or innate tendencies play in their lives. In the final analysis, blood, to me, is so very much thicker than water.

I hope I do not presume when I say I think at the end I really understood my father and appreciated to the full everything he stood for. I may not have shared his sentiments; in fact, sometimes I feel I am now almost anti blood sports; yet, because he was as he was, it seemed entirely right that he should have enjoyed his shooting and fishing so much. When he was about 14 he once remarked to his father how much he would like to go salmon fishing. The latter replied to the effect that there was nothing stopping him, that the world contained all sorts of good things and he was free to help himself by his own efforts. My father was nearly 60 before he achieved his youthful heart's desire and was able to take up this particular form of sport, but when he did so he did it as the result of many years of sheer hard work. He neither wanted nor expected help from anyone else. He once wrote in a diary which he kept for a short time, "There is no substitute for personal dignity, and no standard of personal dignity save independence." He was against subsidies of any kind, and, later on in that same diary, he says, "I doubt whether I shall live to see farmers free again, free to prosper or to go bankrupt, I mean."

There would be no more shooting and fishing now and no more working either. How I wished he could have gone right out whilst doing any of those three things, instead of lying there in bed trying so hard to read. He seemed to have forgotten, thank goodness, the article which he had been unable to write. His secretary, Beryl Davidge, came and went, dealing efficiently with his correspondence, occasionally asking him to sign his name to a cheque. She was a quiet and sympathetic person in whom he placed implicit trust. Once, during the following week, whilst she was guiding his hand in order to write a very shaky signature in the correct place, I heard him say to her, "It seems as if it's all over for me, my dear." When she came out of the room, she was crying.

Yet he never really gave in. He insisted on getting out of bed or sitting up in it, turning his television set on and off with his remote-control switch, learning to use an electric shaver for the first time or peering hard at a book. I asked him if he would like me to read to him, and he nodded and passed me a volume of Kipling's short stories, opened at *An Habitation Enforced*, the story of an American couple who settled in the English countryside, discovering and reclaiming a lost inheritance. It is a beautiful story, implying that the countryman belongs to the land, the landlord to his tenants and the farmer to his labourers and not the other way about. I began to read, but before I had got very far I noticed the tears were streaming down his face. I felt the emotion might be too much for him, and I made some pretext to go out of the room. The wheel had come full circle now, and here was I trying to take up the role, albeit inadequately, which he himself had played when he read *Helen's Babies* to me so many long years ago.

The doctor brought a specialist out from Salisbury, and when they came downstairs after examining him their faces were grave. They talked about age and the furring up of his arteries. My husband asked whether my father ought not to be in hospital, but they shook their heads. They said there was nothing much anyone could do, and it would be better for him to remain quietly at home. We asked what we should do if he fell down, because he was so heavy yet insisted on getting out of bed, and some days he also insisted on coming down to his study. They said we should just have to make him comfortable until we could summon help to get him back to bed again. It was not very encouraging or constructive. They knew, of course, that this was a terminal case. He would never be quite the same again.

The next day he appeared to be worse. I noticed he no longer switched on his television set and he could not manage to eat his boiled egg unaided. There was obviously some kind of disconnection going on in his brain. He asked for a large clock; he could see the hands but he could not tell the time. He kept puzzling over it and our hearts ached for him. Brian came stumping up to the bedroom, trying to cheer him on with good news from the farming front; but we all felt so helpless, my mother, Vivi, Beryl, Brian and I. He had always been so strong; he had always known what to do, and the house had revolved round him. We were like a broken wheel going round in useless circles. The hub was missing. It was all the more distressing because my mother had also been in poor health herself for a number of years.

Some days he seemed to rally. He would say, "Get Brian to bring the Land Rover to the front door. I want to see that field of barley," or "I want to go to the Salisbury Club and play bridge tonight. See that Brian is ready." We made excuses under the plea that the doctors had ordered him to rest and he was not quite fit enough. He began to get angry, and we tried to change the subject.

Some days he came downstairs. We helped him to dress, and he took meticulous care in the selection of a suitable tie. He was pathetically buoyed up when he felt things were getting back to normal. Sitting at his huge desk in his study seemed to comfort him. Then one day, after lunch, he got up from the dining-table and more or less collapsed. The journey back to his bedroom seemed a hundred miles long. . . .

We had to get him to hospital. He could no longer help himself, and he was becoming too heavy to lift, even for Brian. He needed more than one male nurse. When the ambulance men came for my father they slung him in a hammock and carried him downstairs, and he joked with them. They were infinitely gentle. . . .

After they had settled him comfortably, I climbed up into the back of the ambulance, and we drove off very slowly. He looked out of the window at the rolling Wiltshire downs he loved so much and his large field of barley, showing green and full of promise in the late May sunshine. I wondered what he was thinking and how well he could see it, and whether he would be alive when it was harvested. Somehow I did not think so.

He was admitted to a public ward, because there was no private room available for three days. I hated seeing him there, just because it was him. If it had been myself or anyone else it would have been quite all right, but I just did not want my father in a public ward, and once again I began to doubt my Leftish principles. Although he was talking garrulously to the patient next to him, he did not look right there; even the bed he was in did not fit him; it was too short, and his poor feet stuck out at the end.

The doctor, sensing my distress, managed to conjure up a private room the following day, although by then my father had suffered a complete stroke, and he was paralysed all down his left side. I was haunted by the thought that we should either have had him admitted to hospital sooner or somehow managed not to have moved him at all. He kept asking what had happened and where he was. I think they all expected him to die, but by the end of the week he rallied once more. He varied each day; mostly he was very confused, but sometimes he was just my father again. I minded more about his mental state than his poor useless body, with all the contraptions which the doctors had rigged up over his bed in order to deal with it. He had always had such an abundance of plain common sense. No one could say now how long he might go on like this; there was even talk of getting him home again in a wheel-chair.

He received innumerable letters wishing him well, not only from friends but completely unknown people who liked his books or listened to his broadcasts. We read them out to him, and either Beryl or I replied. He liked someone he knew to be near him all the time because he desperately wanted contact with the outside world. He had never been so long without his desk and his telephone, and, although the nurses sometimes wheeled the portable telephone into his room, there were not many days when he was able to use it.

I suppose, in some ways, he was the most difficult patient the hospital had ever dealt with, and yet when he died I do not think there was a nurse who did not grieve for him, especially the older ones. There was one particular auxiliary, quite untrained, of whom he used to say, "Now she's a proper nurse, better than any who have passed examinations. She's got *humanity*."

He had names for them all. On arriving to visit him each day, as I got half way down the passage I would hear him shouting, "Rosy, Budge, Flower, where the devil is everyone?" And then as I came into the room, "Thank God you've come. You don't know what it's like watching that door and waiting for someone to come in." It was curious about his sight because, although he could recognize any of us, he was unable to distinguish between day or night, so that sometimes he got upset at two o'clock in the morning and wanted the night nurse to ring me up to know why I was not there.

As the weeks went by, the doctor wondered whether he might not be happier back in a public ward, where he could see things going on all the time; but, all things being considered, we felt it best that he should remain where he was. My mother, Vivi, Beryl and I tried to be with him as much as we could. I remembered how, before he was ever ill, he often used to come out of his study door after he had finished writing, saying, "Where are my womenfolk? I want some company. It isn't good for a man to be alone."

"Contact, that's what I want," he kept saying now. "All my life I've been able to get contact by just picking up the telephone, and now I'm cut off and at the mercy of all these nurses, who are worked off their feet, poor souls. Take them out and give them a good champagne lunch at my expense."

They gave him physiotherapy. A young woman used to come every day and try to bring some life back into his deadened limbs. But it was no use, and I think we all knew it. He became exhausted, and they had to give up. There was this thing erected over his bed like a small crane, on which he had to be hoisted every time they wanted to move him. He was slung up like a four-bushel sack, one of those heavy sacks, the use of which he had campaigned against so successfully years ago. Someone once asked him what he would like to be remembered for, and he had said, "Well, most cows nowadays are spared the agony of being gnashed by their neighbour's horns, and few people now get ruptures from heaving four-bushel sacks about." The de-horning of cattle and the abolition of the four-bushel sack were subjects on which he wrote and felt most strongly.

He suffered much pain, especially every time the lifting apparatus was used. We were into July. I managed to find a private nurse who could be with him each morning, and we tried to see he was not left by himself the rest of the day. As each evening drew near I found it increasingly hard to leave him, so stricken, so helpless, and so alone.

He was going downhill rapidly; we could all see it. The doctors said he could have anything he wished for. Occasionally I lit a cigar for him, and he had a puff or two, or I helped him to drink a weak whisky and soda. Once or twice I brought his grand-daughter to see him when she was home from boarding-school. Unlike her grandfather, she is musically inclined, and she played her guitar and sang to him, which he seemed to enjoy. I never now listen to "South of the Border" without a very special heartache.

On 16th July I was due to go to her school for Parents' Day and to listen to her playing a solo on the piano in a concert. My father was very weak now, and my loyalties were torn. He had developed a chest infection, but he had a merciful doctor who said, "I do not propose to give him antibiotics."

The Sister telephoned me early that morning and said my father had had one of his surprising rallies and was even demanding some breakfast. I put my best clothes into the back of the car, and my husband and I went to see him. Whilst I was talking to the Sister, my husband told my father about the occasion and what his grand-daughter would be doing, and asked him whether he would mind if I went away for the day. Almost his last coherent words were, "I want her to go. I want her to go very much indeed."

A bevy of excited young things in bright cotton dresses greeted us on our arrival at the school. Mothers wearing gay summer hats strolled across the lawn. The contrast between this scene and the one we had recently left was painfully sharp. Here, there was life and everyone looking forward; behind us, eighty miles away, there could only be a looking back.

I remember little of the concert except the gently-flowing sound of Debussy as my daughter started playing. I was conscious of Time and somehow being in the middle of it with a generation on either side of me. I thought of my father lying there in the hospital and how, many years ago, he too had been a parent at a school performance. I recalled one Christmas term and the pleasure it gave him to watch a one-act play I had written and produced, even though the joke which brought forth the loudest laughter from the entire audience happened to be when a policeman's moustache accidentally fell off half way through the most important scene. Now, as I watched my own child leave the stage, I tried to push aside the thought that her grandfather might no longer be alive when we returned.

On the way home that evening we called in at the hospital. The morning's brightness had been short-lived, and the following day my father became more or less unconscious. He lived another four days, but he was in no pain now. The doctors at least promised us that. During those long hours whilst we waited for the end, one of the night nurses said to me, "You can always tell the ones who have had to fight in life, when it comes to a time like this. They're the ones who keep on longest."

My father, A.G., died just before the start of harvest on Thursday, 21st July, 1966, with the Sister and me beside him. Suddenly, I realized that there would be a lot to do. I must 'keep on keeping on'. . . .

EPITAPH

'Tis hard to have to lie a-bed
Dreamin',
Wi' all the summer's work ahead,
Screamin'
And callin' out fer such as I
To lend a hand 'afore I die,
But 'tis no use; my time be nigh,
Seemin'.

I've watched the barley up on hill
Growin';
I'm gettin' on but I be still
Knowin'.
And I do know as how fer me
There's only one more harvest, see?
My work be done; 'tis right I be
Goin'.

So when I'm took, don't let 'em bide
Weepin'.
Wi' all the rest o' countryside
Reapin'.
Just mind thic barley field up yon,
You get 'un carried when I'm gone;
And leave me be to go right on
Sleepin'.

P.S.

List of Books by A. G. Street

Farmer's Glory
Strawberry Roan
The Endless Furrow
The Gentleman of the Party
A Crook in the Furrow
Already Walks Tomorrow
Holdfast
Shameful Harvest
Wessex Wins
Wheat & Chaff (*comprising Hedgetrimmings, Country Days, & Thinking Aloud*)
Harvest by Lamplight
Feather-Bedding
Farming: How to Begin
Master of None
In His Own Country (*comprising Country Calendar, Moonraking, A Year of My Life, Hitler's Whistle & Ditchampton Farm*)
Landmarks
Round the Year on a Farm
Kittle Kattle
Sweetacres
Bobby Bocker
From Dusk Till Dawn
Farming England
Land Everlasting
Cooper's Crossing
Fish & Chips
Johnny Cowslip